Welcome to the EVERYTHING® series!

THESE HANDY, accessible books give you all you need to tackle a difficult project, gain a new hobby, comprehend a fascinating topic, prepare for an exam, or even brush up on something you learned back in school but have since forgotten.

You can read an *EVERYTHING*® book from cover to cover or just pick out the information you want from our four useful boxes: e-facts, e-ssentials, e-alerts, and e-questions. We literally give you everything you need to know on the subject, but throw in a lot of fun stuff along the way, too.

We now have well over 150 *EVERYTHING*® books in print, spanning such wide-ranging topics as weddings, pregnancy, wine, learning guitar, one-pot cooking, managing people, and so much more. When you're done reading them all, you can finally say you know *EVERYTHING*®!

E FACTS: Important sound bytes of information

E ESSENTIALS: Quick and handy tips

E ALERTS!: Urgent warnings

E QUESTIONS: Solutions to common problems

THE
EVERYTHING®
— Series —

Dear Reader,

Thanks for picking up *The Everything® Spanish Phrase Book*. I hope you're as excited about learning Spanish as I am about sharing this phrase book with you.

I wasn't born speaking Spanish. In fact, I first started studying Spanish in college to prove to someone that I couldn't learn a foreign language! Well, I was wrong. Wasn't I surprised to find that not only could I learn a language, but that I was able to converse in Spanish within a couple of months? That first Spanish class laid a groundwork of grammar and vocabulary that allowed me to become truly fluent only two years later. (Okay, admittedly, that was after living in Spain for a year.) Now, years later, I'm here to spread the *palabra*. Anyone, and I mean *anyone*, can learn a foreign language. All it takes is an open mind, a loose tongue, a good grounding in grammar, plus some practice.

Thanks for taking the journey with me and enjoy the ride!

Cari Luna

THE
EVERYTHING®
SPANISH
PHRASE
BOOK

A quick reference for any situation

Cari Luna

Adams Media
Avon, Massachusetts

For Doña Sofía

An Everything® Series Book.
Everything® and everything.com® are registered trademarks of
F+W Publications, Inc.

Published by Adams Media, an F+W Publications Company
57 Littlefield Street, Avon, MA 02322 U.S.A.
www.adamsmedia.com

ISBN: 1-59337-049-0

Printed in Canada.

J I H G F E D

Library of Congress Cataloging-in-Publication Data
Luna, Cari.
The everything Spanish phrase book/Cari Luna.
p.   cm.
English and Spanish.
ISBN 1-59337-049-0
1. Spanish language—Conversation and phrase books—English.
I. Title: Spanish phrase book. II. Title. III. Series: Everything series.

PC4121.L86 2004
468.3'421–dc22

2003026252

This publication is designed to provide accurate and authoritative information with regard to the subject matter covered. It is sold with the understanding that the publisher is not engaged in rendering legal, accounting,
or other professional advice. If legal advice or other expert assistance is
required, the services of a competent professional person should be sought.
—From a *Declaration of Principles* jointly adopted by a Committee of the
American Bar Association and a Committee of Publishers and Associations

Many of the designations used by manufacturers and sellers to distinguish
their products are claimed as trademarks. Where those designations appear
in this book and Adams Media was aware of a trademark claim, the designations have been printed with initial capital letters.

Cover illustrations by Barry Littmann.

This book is available at quantity discounts for bulk purchases.
For information, call 1-800-872-5627.

THE

EVERYTHING®
Series

EDITORIAL

Publishing Director: Gary M. Krebs
Managing Editor: Kate McBride
Copy Chief: Laura MacLaughlin
Acquisitions Editor: Eric M. Hall
Development Editor: Julie Gutin
Production Editor: Jamie Wielgus
Language Editor: Susana C. Schultz

PRODUCTION

Production Director: Susan Beale
Production Manager: Michelle Roy Kelly
Series Designer: Daria Perreault
Cover Design: Paul Beatrice and Frank Rivera
Layout and Graphics: Colleen Cunningham,
Rachael Eiben, Michelle Roy Kelly,
John Paulhus, Daria Perreault, Erin Ring

Visit the entire Everything® series at www.everything.com

Acknowledgments

Thanks to Billy, who provided infinite amounts of patience, love, and home-cooked spinach burritos while I wrestled to get this book in on deadline.

Thanks to my agent, the mighty Jacky Sach.

Thanks to my editor, the always encouraging and supportive Eric Hall.

Thanks to Julie Gutin, the dedicated and enthusiastic development editor.

Contents

The Top Ten
Spanish Phrases You Should Know

1. **Do you speak English?** *¿Habla usted inglés?*

   AH-blah OO-stehd een-GLEHS

2. **I don't understand.** *No comprendo.*

   noh kohm-PREHN-doh

3. **I'm allergic to** . . . *Soy alérgico/a a* . . .

   sohy ah-LEHR-hee-koh/kah ah

4. **I need a doctor.** *Necesito un doctor.*

   neh-seh-SEE-toh oon dohk-TOHR

5. **Where is the emergency exit?** *¿Dónde está la salida de emergencia?* DOHN-deh eh-STAH lah sah-LEE-dah deh eh-mehr-HEN-see-ah

6. **Hello!** *¡Hola!* OH-lah

7. **Good-bye!** *¡Adiós!* ah-dee-OHS

8. **My name is** . . . *Me llamo* . . . me YAH-moh

9. **Where is** . . . **?** *¿Dónde está* . . . **?**

   DOHN-deh eh-STAH

10. **I'm lost.** *Estoy perdido/a.*

    eh-STOHY pehr-DEE-doh/dah

Introduction

¡Bienvenidos! Welcome to *The Everything® Spanish Phrase Book!* Whether you intend to use this book when traveling to a Spanish-speaking country, or to speak with Spanish-speakers in your community or workplace, here you'll find the tools that will help you to communicate.

If you already have some formal knowledge of Spanish under your belt, you'll appreciate this book as a quick reference or refresher. The thematic organization will make it easy to find the information you're looking for.

No prior experience with Spanish? No problem! You may be surprised to find out how much of the Spanish language you've already absorbed from the world around you. Spanish is everywhere these days. In fact, many words in common usage in American English today have been adopted directly from Spanish. In addition to the Spanish vocabulary you already have, we'll build up your skills in an easy-to-understand way. Don't worry! Anyone can learn a foreign language, with a little bit of patience and a willingness to try. Perhaps along the way you'll even fall in love with this beautiful language, and dedicate yourself to further study of it.

No phrase book can hope to present a language in its entirety. You can use *The Everything® Spanish Phrase Book* as a means of reviewing the basics in anticipation of a trip or other situation that will call for Spanish language skills, or you can carry it with you and refer to it as the need arises. You can start off with a basic intro-duction to Spanish pronunciation and grammar, to get your bearings. You'll find that understanding Spanish grammar will make your communication in Spanish easier and more natural. It'll allow you to take a step away from searching for individual words and phrases and toward true conversation.

The following chapters are organized by vocabulary theme or situation. Each thematic section provides you with the words and phrases you'll need for most typical encounters, from meeting someone for the first time, to travel, dining out, and working together in a business setting. Each vocabulary word and phrase is followed by a transliteration to help you pronounce it properly. You can also refer back to the pronunciation guide in Chapter 1 whenever you need a reminder.

In addition to thematic chapters, there's also a col-lection of must-have words and phrases for basic com-munication, organized into one chapter for quick, at-a-glance reference. Use it on the spot as the need arises, or in combination with the appropriate thematic chapter for more in-depth conversation.

And there's also a chapter that covers idioms, say-ings, and slang to give you a feel for the flavor of everyday conversation in Spanish. While not necessary for navigating the streets of Barcelona, closing a busi-ness deal in Mexico City, or ordering a meal in Miami, having a few idioms and slang words in your arsenal will make it easier to connect with the native speakers around you.

Chapter 1

Pronunciation and Grammar

This chapter is by no means intended to replace formal Spanish instruction or a Spanish textbook. What it will give you is a basic understanding of Spanish pronunciation and grammar, to put the phrases you'll find later in the book into a framework. We hope that this basic introduction will serve you well as you explore the rest of this book. In the next chapter, we jump right into conversation. *¡Buena suerte!* Good luck!

A Guide to Pronunciation

Spanish isn't a difficult language to pronounce. Just remember to relax your mouth and use your lips. We don't really use our lips all that much in English, but you'll need them in Spanish, so don't be afraid to put them out there!

The great thing about Spanish pronunciation is that it sounds exactly the way it's spelled. In English, "car" and "cat" have two different vowel sounds in spite of their similar spellings. In Spanish, the letter "a" always represents one particular sound.

Even more conveniently, there are two simple rules that govern which syllable in any word is normally accented:

1. In words that end in a vowel (–a, –e, –i, –o, –u), "–s," or "–n," the stress normally falls on the second-to-last syllable. For example: *mano* (MAH-noh), hand; *playas* (PLAH-yahs), beaches; *cantaban* (kahn-TAH-bahn), they sang.
2. In words that end in any consonant except "–s" or "–n," the stress normally falls on the last syllable. For example: *verdad* (vehr-DAHD), truth; *azul* (ah-SOOL), blue; *luz* (loos), light.

However, some words don't follow these two rules. To let the readers know how these words should be stressed in pronunciation, Spanish employs an acute accent mark (´) over the vowel to indicate the stressed syllable. For example: *lápiz* (LAH-pees), pencil; *médico*

(MEH-dee-coh), doctor; *música* (MOO-see-kah), music. The accent mark might also be used to differentiate two words with same spelling but different meaning: *dónde* (DOHN-deh), where (question word); *donde* (DOHN-deh), where (as a preposition).

 ESSENTIAL

Just as with English, there is a wide variety of accents in the Spanish language because it's spoken in so many different countries and cultures throughout the world. Because it's impossible to cover them all, this book presents the pronunciations you're most likely to hear coming from people from Central and South America.

The Pronunciation Guide chart will certainly help you with pronunciation, but nothing works as well as getting the sound of the language in your ear. To learn to pronounce Spanish words, listen to the spoken language. Listening to Spanish on TV, the radio, or the city bus will get your ear accustomed to the sounds, and you'll find it much easier to recreate them yourself.

Pronunciation Guide

Letter	Sound	Example	Pronunciation
a	ah	*ala* (wing)	AH-la
b	b	*bolsa* (bag)	BOHL-sah
c	s before i, e; k in all other cases	*centro* (center), *casa* (house)	SEHN-troh, KAH-sah
ch	ch	*coche* (car)	KOH-cheh
d	d	*dedo* (finger)	DEH-do
e	eh	*estar* (to be)	eh-STAHR
f	f	*falso* (false)	FAHL-soh
g	a hard h sound before e, i; a hard g sound in all other cases	*gente* (people), *gracias* (thanks)	HEHN-the, GRAH-see-ahs
h	silent	*hola* (hi)	OH-lah
i	ee	*igual* (equal)	ee-GWAHL
j	a hard h	*jabón* (soap)	hah-BOHN
k	k in words of foreign origin	*kilo* (kilogram)	KEE-loh
l	l	*lado* (side)	LAH-doh
ll	y	*llamar* (to call)	yah-MAHR
m	m	*muy* (very)	mui
n	n	*nunca* (never)	NUHN-kah
ñ	ny	*mañana* (tomorrow)	mah-NYAH-nah
o	oh	*ojo* (eye)	OH-hoh
p	p	*pelo* (hair)	PEH-loh
q	k	*quince* (fifteen)	KEEN-seh

r	a hard *r*	*radio* (radio)	RAH-dee-oh
rr	a rolled *r*	*perro* (dog)	PEH-rroh
s	s	*sol* (sun)	sohl
t	t	*todo* (all)	TOH-doh
u	oo	*útil* (useful)	OO-tihl
v	v	*vivo* (alive)	VEE-voh
w	*w* in words of foreign origin	*whisky* (whisky)	WEES-kih
x	ks	*éxito* (success)	EHKS-ee-toh
y	y	*yerno* (son-in-law)	YEHR-noh
z	s	*plaza* (square)	PLAH-sah

 ALERT!

You might notice that speakers of Spanish pronounce "v" so that it sounds more like "b." Don't worry, you're not hearing things. This is a common speech modification found in several languages.

The *u*, which is usually pronounced as *oo*, presents a challenge when it follows the letter *g*. If the combination *gu* is followed by *a* it's always pronounced like *oo*— *guardia* (policeman) GWAHR-dee-ah. If it's followed by *e* or *i* it's silent, and it's only pronounced as oo when it carries the umlaut (¨): *nicaragüense* (Nicaraguan) is pronounced nee-cah-rah-GWEHN-seh.

The Spanish You Already Know

Now that you've gotten a quick introduction to Spanish pronunciation, it's time to go on to Spanish vocabulary. Fortunately, you already know more Spanish than you probably realize, because English and Spanish share many cognates—words that share a similar meaning and spelling because they originated from the same word. Study the cognates provided here, and you'll have a head start on building a strong Spanish vocabulary.

Cognates

Spanish	English
actor	*actor*
	ahk-TOHR
animal	*animal*
	ah-nee-MAHL
apart	*aparte*
	ah-PAHR-teh
appreciation	*apreciación*
	ah-preh-see-ah-see-OHN
banana	*banana*
	bah-NAH-nah
biography	*biografía*
	bee-oh-grah-FEE-ah
color	*color*
	koh-LOHR
comfortable	*confortable*
	kohn-fohr-TAH-bleh
cruel	*cruel*
	kroo-EHL

dictionary	*diccionario*
	deek-see-ohn-AH-ree-oh
family	*familia*
	fah-MEE-lee-ah
grave (serious)	*grave*
	GRAH-veh
horrible	*horrible*
	oh-RREE-bleh
hospital	*hospital*
	hohs-pee-TAHL
hotel	*hotel*
	oh-TEHL
music	*música*
	MOO-see-kah
natural	*natural*
	nah-too-RAHL
opinion	*opinión*
	oh-pee-NYOHN
origin	*origen*
	oh-REE-hen
park (noun)	*parque*
	PAHR-keh
possible	*posible*
	poh-SEE-bleh
radio	*radio*
	RAH-dee-oh
resist	*resistir*
	reh-sees-TEER
restaurant	*restaurante*
	rehs-taoo-RAHN-teh

Cognates (continued)

revision	*revisión*
	reh-vee-see-OHN
revolution	*revolución*
	reh-voh-loo-see-OHN
ritual	*ritual*
	ree-too-AHL
tropical	*tropical*
	troh-pee-KAHL
university	*universidad*
	oo-nee-vehr-see-DAHD

Beware the False Friend!

Don't assume a word is a cognate just because it sounds like an English word you know. Some words *look* and *sound* like they should be cognates, but they aren't—they actually mean two different things in two different languages. Misuse some of these false cognates, and the results could be rather embarrassing.

Common False Cognates

actual	current
ahk-too-AHL	
asistir	to attend
ah-sees-TEEHR	
atender	to serve
ah-tehn-DEHR	
compromiso	commitment
kohm-proh-MEE-soh	

decepción	disappointment
deh-sehp-see-OHN	
embarazada	pregnant
ehm-bah-rah-SAH-dah	
éxito	success
EHK-see-toh	
largo	long
LAHR-goh	
molestar	to bother
moh-lehs-TAHR	
pretender	to try
preh-tehn-DEHR	
recordar	to remember
reh-kohr-DAHR	
ropa	clothing
ROH-pah	
sano	healthy
SAH-noh	
simpático	nice
seem-PAH-tee-koh	

Now that you've gotten a bit of pronunciation practice and started to build a bit of vocabulary, the next step is a quick introduction to Spanish grammar.

Nouns and Articles

In Spanish, just as in English, nouns are words for people, places, and things. The difference in Spanish, however, is that each noun has a gender: It is either masculine or feminine. The gender of the noun will determine what article it takes.

 FACT

> English only has three articles: "a" and "an" (indefinite articles), and "the" (a definite article). Spanish also has definite and indefinite articles, but they vary according to the gender and number of the noun.

In the Singular

For example, *bolígrafo* is the Spanish word for "pen." It's masculine, so to say "the pen" we would use the masculine article *el*. On the other hand, *casa* (house) is a feminine noun. To say "the house" we would use the feminine article *la*. For indefinite articles, use *un* for masculine nouns and *una* for feminine nouns.

Singular Spanish Articles

el	ehl	the (masculine)
la	lah	the (feminine)
un	oon	a (masculine)
una	OO-nah	a (feminine)

How do you know which nouns are masculine and which are feminine? Generally, masculine nouns end with –*o*, and feminine nouns end with –*a*. Of course, there are exceptions, which will have to be memorized.

Don't worry, though! Mistakes with the gender of a noun are common, and you'll still be understood. As long as you're aware that there is such a thing as noun gender, there's no need to agonize over it. As you become more familiar with the language, the correct article will come to you naturally.

In the Plural

Just as in English, a Spanish noun is made plural by adding either *-s* or *-es* to the singular form. However, in Spanish, the articles that accompany the nouns also have singular and plural forms and still retain their gender differences. For example, *el bolígrafo* becomes *los bolígrafos*; *la casa* becomes *las casas*.

 ESSENTIAL

> Adjectives modify nouns. In Spanish, adjectives are conjugated just as articles—the ending changes based on the gender and number of the noun. For example, look at the conjugations of pequeño (little): *la casa pequeña, las casas pequeñas, el bolígrafo pequeño, los bolígrafos pequeños*. Also note that in Spanish, adjectives generally follow the nouns they describe.

There's also a difference in the use of indefinite articles in the plural. In English, we drop "a" or "an" when the noun is plural, whereas in Spanish, the articles *un* and *una* are made plural and may be translated as "some." So, "(some) pens" are *unos bolígrafos* and "(some) houses" are *unas casas.*

Plural Spanish Articles

los	lohs	the (masculine)
las	lahs	the (feminine)
unos	OO-nohs	some (masculine)
unas	OO-nahs	some (feminine)

From Noun to Pronoun

A pronoun is a word that takes the place of a noun. Subject pronouns are not used as often in spoken Spanish as in English, because they are implied by the verb ending used. For example, it would be correct to say: *yo soy americana* (I am American). However, what you're much more likely to hear in actual conversation is: *soy americana.* Because *soy* is the first-person singular conjugation of the verb *ser* (to be), the "I" is clear even without the pronoun.

Personal Subject Pronouns

yo	yoh	I
tú	too	you (singular, informal)
usted	oo-STEHD	you (singular, formal)
él	ehl	he
ella	EHY-yah	she
nosotros	noh-SOH-trohs	we

nosotras	noh-SOH-trahs	we (feminine)
vosotros	voh-SOH-trohs	you (plural, used in Spain)
vosotras	voh-SOH-trahs	you (plural, feminine, used in Spain)
ustedes	oo-STEH-dehs	you (plural)
ellos	EHY-yohs	they
ellas	EHY-yahs	they (feminine)

You and You

So when do you use *tú* and when do you use *usted*? When addressing one person, you need to choose either the formal *(usted)* or the informal *(tú)* way of saying "you." If you are speaking to a child or a friend, use the *tú* form. Otherwise, it's best to err on the side of formality and use *usted*.

And what about *vosotros* and *ustedes*? The distinction is easy—you'll only hear *vosotros* used in Spain. For the most part, the rest of the Spanish-speaking world uses *ustedes* for the plural form of "you," whether the address is formal or informal. If you are in Spain, the guidelines for choosing between *vosotros* and *ustedes* are the same as those for *tú* and *usted*—it depends on the degree of formality.

Be aware that because there are informal and formal ways of addressing people, these distinctions do carry meaning. For example, if you normally use *tú* with a friend and then switch to *usted*, you may be expressing anger or a desire to distance yourself from that person. Similarly, if you use *tú* when addressing an older person or one in a position of respect, such as a judge or police officer, then that choice indicates intentional disrespect.

Verbs and Conjugation

A verb is a word that shows action. Verbs need to be conjugated to express who is doing the action and when it's being done. Regular Spanish verbs are conjugated by dropping the infinitive ending (*–ar*, *–er*, or *–ir*) and attaching the appropriate ending. Most of the verbs in this book are in the present tense—other tenses are beyond the scope of this phrase book. If this is a topic that interests you, we encourage you to seek more in-depth Spanish language instruction or pick up *The Everything® Spanish Verb Book*.

Regular Verb Endings

Subject Pronoun	*–ar*	*–er*	*–ir*
yo	*–o*	*–o*	*–o*
tú	*–as*	*–es*	*–es*
él, ella, usted	*–a*	*–e*	*–e*
nosotros, nosotras	*–amos*	*–emos*	*–imos*
vosotros, vosotras	*–áis*	*–éis*	*–ís*
ellos, ellas, ustedes	*–an*	*–en*	*–en*

Here are three sample conjugations of regular verbs.

BUSCAR: to look for (*–ar* verb)

yo busco (BOO-skoh)

tú buscas (BOO-skahs)

él, ella, usted busca (BOO-skah)

nosotros buscamos (boo-SKAH-mohs)

vosotros buscáis (boo-SKAHYS)

ellos, ellas, ustedes buscan (BOO-skahn)

VENDER: to sell (*–er* verb)

yo vendo (VEHN-doh)

tú vendes (VEHN-dehs)

él, ella, usted vende (VEHN-deh)

nosotros vendemos (vehn-DEH-mohs)

vosotros vendéis (vehn-DEHYS)

ellos, ellas, ustedes venden (VEHN-dehn)

VIVIR: to live (*–ir* verb)

yo vivo (VEE-vo)

tú vives (VEE-vehs)

él, ella, usted vive (VEE-veh)

nosotros vivimos (vee-VEE-mohs)

vosotros vivís (vee-VEES)

ellos, ellas, ustedes viven (VEE-vehn)

Irregular verb conjugations vary from this format. They might have modified spelling to accommodate correct pronunciation, or they might sound markedly different from the infinitive. Irregular verb conjugations need to be memorized.

IR: to go (irregular)

yo voy (voy)
tú vas (vahs)
él, ella, usted va (vah)
nosotros vamos (vAH-mohs)
vosotros vais (vahys)
ellos, ellas, ustedes van (vahn)

Reflexive Verbs

A reflexive verb is one that describes an action that the subject takes upon itself. An example of a reflexive verb is *llamarse*, literally "to call oneself." In Spanish, this verb is used to say "my name is . . ."

Yo me llamo Susan.
My name is Susan.

Tú te llamas Roberto.
Your name is Robert.

Reflexive Pronouns

me	meh	myself
te	teh	yourself (singular, informal)
se	seh	himself, herself, yourself, themselves, yourselves
nos	nohs	ourselves
os	ohs	yourselves (plural, informal in Spain)

Chapter 2
Introduce Yourself

Learning a language is about communication. It's about connecting with the people around you, whether you're on vacation or in your own hometown. At home or abroad, if you want to have a friendly conversation, you need to know how to greet people appropriately, how to introduce and describe yourself, and how to ask them about others in a polite manner.

Before You Begin

Before you plunge right into conversation with that friendly woman standing in line in front of you, there are a few rules to keep in mind:

- **Be polite.** Remember that there are two different ways of addressing a person in Spanish—by using *tú* or *usted*. This matters more in some Spanish-speaking countries and cultures than others, but when in doubt use the more formal *usted*.
- **Speak up.** Make an effort to use proper pronunciation so your listeners can understand you more easily.
- **Don't be afraid.** The only way you'll learn is by making mistakes. As a non-native speaker, you will be given more leeway with grammar, and your efforts will definitely be appreciated!

If you don't understand something, or if someone is speaking too quickly, don't get embarrassed and pretend you understood! The goal is communication, right? For the most part, people will be happy to repeat themselves, understanding that you aren't a native speaker. Here are two phrases to help you communicate:

Please repeat.
Repita, por favor.
reh-PEE-tah pohr-fah-VOHR

Please speak more slowly.
Hable más despacio, por favor.
HAH-bleh mahs dehs-PAH-see-yoh pohr-fah-VOHR

Ser or Estar?

There are two different forms of the verb "to be" in Spanish: *ser* and *estar.* If you do accidentally choose the wrong one, chances are you'll still be understood. There are a few instances, however, where making the wrong choice can change the meaning of your statement—sometimes in a rather embarrassing way. It can mean the difference between saying someone is good—*Carmen es buena*—and saying someone has a "good body"—*Carmen está buena.* Ladies, if you're walking down the street and hear someone yelling, *"¡Ay, mami, qué buena estás!"* he doesn't mean you look like a nice person. He's using a *piropo*, which translates as "compliment" but may feel more like a catcall.

 QUESTION?

Not sure when to use *ser* and when to use *estar*?
Keep this in mind: If it's something more or less permanent, like birthplace, nationality, or a physical characteristic, use *ser.* If it's something that changes, like being tired or hungry or lost, use *estar.*

SER: to be

yo soy (soy)

tú eres (EH-rehs)

él, ella, usted es (ehs)

nosotros somos (SOH-mohs)

vosotros sois (soys)

ellos, ellas, ustedes son (sohn)

ESTAR: to be (located)

yo estoy (ehs-TOY)

tú estás (ehs-TAHS)

él, ella, usted está (ehs-TAH)

nosotros estamos (ehs-TAH-mohs)

vosotros estáis (ehs-TAHYS)

ellos, ellas, ustedes están (ehs-TAHN)

Choosing between *ser* and *estar* trips up a lot of people, but it doesn't have to be complicated if you know the basics. The verb *ser* is used to express the following:

- **Nationality, origin, or a permanent characteristic:**
  Soy americana. I'm American.
  Jennifer es de Inglaterra. Jennifer is from England.
  Juan es bajo. Juan is short.

- **A characteristic or condition that will probably be the same for a long period of time:**
  Ellos son abogados. They are lawyers.

- **Date and time:**
  Mi cumpleaños es el veinte de agosto. My birthday is August 20th.
  Son las dos. It's two o'clock.

The verb *estar* is used to express the following:

- **Location:**
  Estoy aquí. I'm here.
  El coche está en el garaje. The car is in the garage.

- **A temporary condition:**
  Linda está cansada. Linda is tired.

Greetings and Farewells

Now that you've got the two "to be" verbs figured out, it's time to make your introductions. The following table presents some words and phrases for greetings, introductions, responses, and farewells.

Greetings and Responses

Hello	*Hola*
	OH-lah
Good morning	*Buenos días*
	BWEH-nos DEE-yahs
Good afternoon	*Buenas tardes*
	BWEH-nas TAHR-dehs
Good evening	*Buenas noches*
	BWEH-nas NOH-ches

Greetings and Responses (continued)

Mr./sir	*Señor*
	seh-NYOHR
Mrs./madam	*Señora*
	seh-NYOH-rah
Miss	*Señorita*
	seh-nyoh-REE-tah

My name is . . .
Me llamo . . .
meh YAH-moh

What is your name?
¿Cómo se llama?
KOH-moh seh YAH-mah

Nice to meet you.
Mucho gusto.
MOO-choh GOO-stoh

 ALERT!

> Note that when you say "nice to meet you,"
> *mucho gusto* is the most common response,
> with the following two responses being
> more formal.

It's a pleasure to meet you.
Es un placer conocerlo/a.
ehs oon plah-SER coh-noh-SEHR-loh/lah

I'm enchanted to meet you.
Encantado/a de conocerlo/a.
ehn-cahn-TAH-doh/dah deh coh-noh-SEHR-loh/lah

Pardon, I didn't catch your name.
Perdón, no escuché su nombre.
pehr-DOHN, noh ehs-coo-CHAY soo NOHM-breh.

How are you?
¿Cómo está usted?
KOH-moh ehs-TAH oo-STEHD

Very well. So-so.
Muy bien. Más o menos.
MOO-ee bee-EHN; mahs oh MEH-nohs

Saying Goodbye

Goodbye	*Adiós*
	ah-dee-OHS
Until later.	*Hasta luego.*
	AH-stah loo-EH-goh
Until tomorrow.	*Hasta mañana.*
	AH-stah mah-NYAH-nah

Introducing Others

If friends or family are with you, you'll certainly want to include them in the conversation. Introduce them as follows: *Este/a es mi . . .* (EH-steh/stah ehs mee), which means "This is my . . ."

Family Members

wife	*esposa*
	ehs-POH-sah
husband	*esposo, marido*
	ehs-POH-soh, mah-REE-doh
girlfriend	*novia*
	NOH-vee-ah
boyfriend	*novio*
	NOH-vee-oh
fiancé(e)	*prometido/a*
	proh-meh-TEE-doh/dah
daughter	*hija*
	EE-hah
son	*hijo*
	EE-hoh
mother	*madre*
	MAH-dreh
father	*padre*
	PAH-dreh
sister	*hermana*
	ehr-MAH-nah
brother	*hermano*
	ehr-MAH-noh
grandmother	*abuela*
	ah-BWEH-lah

grandfather	*abuelo*
	ah-BWEH-loh
aunt	*tía*
	TEE-ah
uncle	*tío*
	TEE-oh
cousin	*primo/a*
	PREE-moh/mah
niece	*sobrina*
	soh-BREE-nah
nephew	*sobrino*
	soh-BREE-noh
stepmother	*madrastra*
	mah-DRAHS-trah
stepfather	*padrastro*
	pah-DRAHS-troh
stepdaughter	*hijastra*
	ee-HAS-trah
stepson	*hijastro*
	ee-HAS-troh
stepsister	*hermanastra*
	ehr-mah-NAHS-trah
stepbrother	*hermanastro*
	ehr-mah-NAHS-troh
granddaughter	*nieta*
	nee-EH-tah
grandson	*nieto*
	nee-EH-toh
mother-in-law	*suegra*
	SWEH-grah

Family Members (continued)

father-in-law	*suegro*
	SWEH-groh
sister-in-law	*cuñada*
	koo-NYAH-dah
brother-in-law	*cuñado*
	koo-NYAH-doh

Friends, Coworkers, and Others

friend	*amigo/a*
	ah-MEE-goh/gah
neighbor	*vecino/a*
	veh-SEE-noh/nah
boss	*jefe/a*
	HEH-feh/fah
coworker	*colega*
	koh-LEH-gah

 ALERT!

The use of the familiar *tú* and the formal *usted* varies widely from country to country, and even from region to region within countries. Err on the side of caution—it's best to begin by using *usted*, and then take your cue from the native speakers around you.

Getting to Know You

Now that everyone's been introduced, you'll want to share some information about yourself and learn more about the person you've just met.

Nationality and Origin

You'll recall that the verb *ser* can be used to describe nationality. For example:

Soy americana.
I'm American.

Now, bear in mind that people from Mexico, Central America, and South America are all Americans too! To be clear (and sensitive to this fact), you could also say:

Soy de los Estados Unidos.
soy deh lohs ehs-TAH-dohs oo-NEE-dohs
I'm from the United States.

Soy estadounidense.
soy ehs-tah-doh-oo-nee-DEHN-seh
I'm American (from United States).

Nationalities

American	*americano/a*
	ah-mehr-ee-CAH-noh/nah
Argentinean	*argentino/a*
	ahr-hen-TEE-noh/nah

Nationalities (continued)

Australian	*australiano/a*
	ow-strah-lee-AH-noh/nah
Canadian	*canadiense*
	cah-nah-dee-YEHN-seh
Chilean	*chileno/a*
	chee-LEH-noh/ah
Colombian	*colombiano/a*
	coh-lohm-bee-AH-noh/nah
Costa Rican	*costarricense*
	coh-stah-rree-SEHN-seh
Cuban	*cubano/a*
	coo-BAH-noh/nah
Danish	*danés/esa*
	dah-NEHS/NEHS-ah
Dominican	*dominicano/a*
	doh-mee-nee-CAH-noh/nah
Ecuadorian	*ecuatoriano/a*
	eh-cwah-toh-ree-AH-noh/nah
Egyptian	*egipcio/a*
	eh-HEEP-see-oh/ah
English	*inglés*
	een-GLEHS
European	*europeo/a*
	eh-oo-roh-PEH-oh/ah
French	*francés/a*
	frahn-SEHS/SEHS-ah
German	*alemán/ana*
	ah-leh-MAHN/MAHN-ah
Honduran	*hondureño/a*
	ohn-doo-REH-nyoh/nyah

Iranian	*iraní* ee-RAH-nee
Iraqi	*iraquí* ee-RAH-kee
Irish	*irlandés/esa* eer-lahn-DEHS/DEHS-ah
Italian	*italiano/a* ee-tahl-ee-AH-noh/nah
Mexican	*mexicano/a* meh-hee-CAH-noh/ah
Dutch	*holandés/esa* oh-lahn-DEHS/DEHS-ah
Nicaraguan	*nicaragüense* nee-cah-rah-GWEN-seh
North American	*norteamericano/a* nohr-teh-ah-mehr-ee-CAH-noh/nah
Norwegian	*noruego/a* nohr-WEH-goh/gah
Paraguayan	*paraguayo/a* pah-rah-GOOAH-yoh/ah
Peruvian	*peruano/a* peh-roo-AH-noh/nah
Polish	*polaco/a* poh-LAH-coh/cah
Puerto Rican	*puertorriqueño/a* pwehr-toh-rree-KEH-nyoh/nyah
Filipino/a	*filipino/a* fee-lee-PEE-noh/nah
Russian	*ruso/a* ROO-soh/sah

Nationalities (continued)

El Salvadoran	*salvadoreño/a*
	sahl-vah-doh-REH-nyoh/nyah
South American	*sudamericano/a*
	sood-ah-meh-ree-CAH-noh/nah
Spanish	*español/a*
	eh-spah-NYOHL/NYOHL-ah
Uruguayan	*uruguayo/a*
	oo-roo-GOOAHY-oh/ah
Venezuelan	*venezolano/a*
	veh-neh-soh-LAH-noh/nah

You can also ask what country someone is from:

¿De dónde es usted?
deh DOHN-deh ehs oos-TEHD

The answer is, *Soy de . . .* (soy deh)—I am from . . .

 ESSENTIAL

Most nouns change ending with gender, such as editor: *redactor* for a man, *redactora* for a woman. However, some nouns stay in the same form, regardless of gender of the subject (only the article changes). For example: a male dentist is *un dentista*; a female dentist is *una dentista*.

Countries

America	*América*
	ah-MEH-ree-cah
Argentina	*Argentina*
	ahr-hehn-TEE-nah
Australia	*Australia*
	ow-STRAH-lee-ah
Canada	*Canadá*
	cah-nah-DAH
Chile	*Chile*
	CHEE-leh
Colombia	*Colombia*
	coh-LOHM-bee-ah
Costa Rica	*Costa Rica*
	COH-stah REE-cah
Cuba	*Cuba*
	COO-bah
Denmark	*Dinamarca*
	dee-nah-MAHR-cah
Dominican Republic	*República Dominicana*
	reh-POO-blee-cah
	doh-mee-nee-CAHN-ah
Ecuador	*Ecuador*
	EH-kwah-dohr
Egypt	*Egipto*
	eh-HEEP-toh
England	*Inglaterra*
	een-glah-TEH-rrah
Europe	*Europa*
	eh-oo-ROH-pah

Countries (continued)

France	*Francia*	FRAHN-see-ah
Germany	*Alemania*	ah-leh-MAHN-ee-ah
Honduras	*Honduras*	ohn-DOO-rahs
Iran	*Irán*	ee-RAHN
Iraq	*Irak*	ee-RAHK
Ireland	*Irlanda*	eer-LAHN-dah
Italy	*Italia*	ee-TAH-lee-ah
Mexico	*México*	MEH-hee-koh
the Netherlands	*los Países Bajos*	lohs pah-YEE-sehs BAH-hohs
Nicaragua	*Nicaragua*	nee-cah-RAH-gooah
North America	*América del Norte*	ah-MEH-ree-cah dehl NOHR-teh
Norway	*Noruega*	nohr-WEH-gah
Paraguay	*Paraguay*	pah-rah-GOOAHY
Peru	*Perú*	peh-ROO

Poland	*Polonia*
	poh-LOH-nee-ah
Puerto Rico	*Puerto Rico*
	PWEHR-toh REE-coh
the Philippines	*las Filipinas*
	lahs fee-lee-PEE-nahs
Russia	*Rusia*
	ROO-see-ah
El Salvador	*El Salvador*
	ehl sahl-vah-DOHR
South America	*Sudamérica/América del Sur*
	sood-ah-MEH-ree-cah/ah-MEH-ree-cah dehl soor
Spain	*España*
	eh-SPAH-nyah
United Kingdom	*Reino Unido*
	REY-noh oo-NEE-doh
United States	*Estados Unidos*
	eh-STAH-dohs oo-NEE-dohs
Uruguay	*Uruguay*
	oo-roo-GOOAHY
Venezuela	*Venezuela*
	veh-neh-SWEH-lah

Jobs and Professions

The Spanish verb "to work" is *trabajar* (trah-bah-HAHR), a regular –*ar* verb. And the verb for stating what you are (professionally) is *ser*. For example: *Soy escritora*. I'm a writer.

Professions

accountant	*contador/a* kohn-tah-DOHR/DOHR-ah
actor	*actor/actriz* ahk-TOHR/ahk-TREEHS
artist	*artista* ahr-TEE-stah
dancer	*bailarín/ina* bahy-lah-REEN/REEN-ah
dentist	*dentista* dehn-TEE-stah
doctor	*médico/a* MEH-dee-coh/cah
editor	*redactor/a* reh-dahk-TOHR/TOHR-ah
engineer	*ingeniero/a* een-heh-nee-YEH-roh/rah
firefighter	*bombero/a* bohm-BEH-roh/rah
jeweler	*joyero/a* hoh-YEH-roh/rah
journalist	*periodista* peh-ree-oh-DEE-stah
lawyer	*abogado/a* ah-boh-GAH-doh/dah
manager	*gerente* heh-REHN-teh
mechanic	*mecánico/a* meh-CAH-nee-coh/cah

musician	*músico/a*
	MOO-see-coh/cah
nurse	*enfermero/a*
	ehn-fehr-MEH-roh/rah
painter	*pintor/a*
	peen-TOHR/TOHR-ah
pharmacist	*farmacéutico/a*
	fahr-mah-SEHOO-tee-coh/cah
police officer	*agente de policía*
	ah-HEN-teh deh poh-lee-SEE-yah
postal worker	*cartero/a*
	kahr-TEH-roh/rah
sailor	*marinero/a*
	mah-ree-NEH-roh/rah
salesperson	*vendedor/a*
	vehn-deh-DOHR/DOHR-ah
secretary	*secretario/a*
	seh-kreh-TAH-ree-oh/ah
singer	*cantante*
	kahn-TAHN-teh
soldier	*soldado*
	sohl-DAH-doh
student	*estudiante*
	eh-stoo-dee-AHN-teh
teacher	*profesor/a*
	proh-feh-SOHR/SOHR-ah
waiter, waitress	*camarero/a*
	kah-mah-REH-roh/rah
writer	*escritor/a*
	eh-scree-TOHR/TOHR-ah

As you've seen in this chapter, basic conversation in Spanish isn't difficult. Just combine the simple rules of grammar with the vocabulary provided, and you'll have no problem communicating in Spanish. The following chapter provides more basics you'll be glad you learned once you get out there and start conversing.

 FACT

Spanish is a Romance language, which means it's based on Latin. If you already have a working knowledge of another Romance language, such as Italian or French, you'll find much of Spanish familiar and easy to learn.

Chapter 3
A Day at a Time

What day is today? Where is my hotel room? When will the museum be open? How is the weather? This chapter presents the vocabulary you need to help you get the answers to these basic questions—and many others—and prepare you to start communicating in Spanish.

Count on It

Spanish numbers aren't hard to learn. You'll notice there's a pattern to them, just as there is in English. All you have to do is remember that pattern. For example, in English the word for 21 is a combination of "twenty" and "one." Same in Spanish, where 21 is *veintiuno* (*veinte* and *uno*). It really is that simple! Take a look at the following chart. You'll master numbers in no time.

Counting (Cardinal) Numbers

0	*cero*
	SEH-roh
1	*uno*
	OO-noh
2	*dos*
	dohs
3	*tres*
	trehs
4	*cuatro*
	KWAH-troh
5	*cinco*
	SEEN-koh
6	*seis*
	sehys
7	*siete*
	see-EH-teh
8	*ocho*
	OH-choh
9	*nueve*
	noo-EH-veh

10	*diez*
	dee-EHS
11	*once*
	OHN-seh
12	*doce*
	DOH-seh
13	*trece*
	TREH-seh
14	*catorce*
	kah-TOHR-seh
15	*quince*
	KEEN-seh
16	*dieciséis (diez y seis)*
	dee-ehs-ee-SEHYS
17	*diecisiete*
	dee-ehs-ee-see-EH-teh
18	*dieciocho*
	dee-ehs-ee-OH-choh
19	*diecinueve*
	dee-ehs-ee-noo-EH-veh
20	*veinte*
	VEYN-teh
21	*veintiuno (veinte y uno)*
	veyn-tee-OO-noh
22	*veintidós*
	veyn-tee-DOHS
23	*veintitrés*
	veyn-tee-TREHS
24	*veinticuatro*
	veyn-tee-KWAH-troh

Counting (Cardinal) Numbers (continued)

25	*veinticinco*
	veyn-tee-SEEN-koh
26	*veintiséis*
	veyn-tee-SEHYS
27	*veintisiete*
	veyn-tee-see-EH-teh
28	*veintiocho*
	veyn-tee-OH-choh
29	*veintinueve*
	veyn-tee-noo-EH-veh
30	*treinta*
	TREHYN-tah
40	*cuarenta*
	kwah-REHN-tah
50	*cincuenta*
	seen-KWEHN-tah
60	*sesenta*
	seh-SEHN-tah
70	*setenta*
	seh-TEHN-tah
80	*ochenta*
	oh-CHEN-tah
90	*noventa*
	noh-VEHN-tah
100	*cien*
	see-EHN
101	*ciento uno*
	see-EHN-toh OO-noh

200	*doscientos*	
	doh-see-EHN-tohs	
300	*trescientos*	
	treh-see-EHN-tohs	
400	*cuatrocientos*	
	kwah-troh-see-EHN-tohs	
500	*quinientos*	
	kee-nee-EHN-tohs	
1,000	*mil*	
	meel	
2,000	*dos mil*	
	dohs meel	
10,000	*diez mil*	
	dee-EHS meel	
100,000	*cien mil*	
	see-EHN meel	
1,000,000	*un millón*	
	oon mee-YOHN	
2,000,000	*dos millones*	
	dohs mee-YOHN-ehs	

First, Second, and So On

So let's say you are traveling and after registering at a hotel you need to find out where your room is. You ask, *¿Dónde está mi cuarto?* (DOHN-deh ehs-TAH mee KWAHR-toh). The answer might be, *En el segundo piso*— on the second floor. In this example, "second" is an ordinal number, because it describes the numerical order of the noun.

Ordinal numbers are adjectives, and that means they have to agree with the noun they modify. That is, your room may be on the *segundo piso*, but your second-born daughter would be your *segunda hija*. The following table presents the singular masculine forms.

Ordinal Numbers

first	*primero*
	pree-MEHR-oh
second	*segundo*
	seh-GOON-doh
third	*tercero*
	tehr-SEH-roh
fourth	*cuarto*
	KWAHR-toh
fifth	*quinto*
	KEEN-toh
sixth	*sexto*
	SEX-toh
seventh	*séptimo*
	SEHP-tee-moh
eight	*octavo*
	ohk-TAH-voh
ninth	*noveno*
	noh-VEH-noh
tenth	*décimo*
	DEH-see-moh

Note that in everyday Spanish, ordinal numbers higher than "tenth" are rarely used, so you may hear someone say, *Mi cuarto está en el piso doce.* (My room is on floor twelve.) Sure, you COULD say your room is on *el duodécimo piso*, but it would sound a bit odd.

 FACT

> Sentence construction in Spanish is more flexible than in English. There are two ways to form a question in Spanish. You can either begin the sentence with an interrogative word such as "when", "where", "how", etc., or you can simply form the sentence as you would a statement, but raise your voice at the end to indicate that you're asking a question.

Telling Time

Okay, so you've learned your numbers in Spanish. Now what? One of the handy things you can do with this newfound knowledge is telling time, or more likely, understand the answer when you ask a Spanish-speaker what time it is. Remember that you need to use the verb *ser* when talking about time.

Asking *¿Qué hora es?* (What time is it?) literally means, "What hour is it?" That means that the verb in the answer needs to agree with the number of hours that it is:

Es la una.
It's one o'clock.

Son las dos.
It's two o'clock.

It's also common for people to use the expression *¿Qué horas son?* This is equally correct. Note also that the hour of day is a feminine noun and so takes the feminine article *la*.

 ALERT!

> Remember that verbs must agree with nouns, even when telling time. So, "it's one o'clock" is *es la una*, but "it's two o'clock" is *son las dos*.

Time of Day
Here are some model phrases for telling the time of day:

It's noon.
Es el mediodía.
ehs ehl meh-dee-oh-DEE-ah

It's midnight.
Es la medianoche.
ehs lah meh-dee-ah-NOH-cheh

It's 1:00.
Es la una.
ehs lah OO-nah

It's 2:00.
Son las dos.
sohn lahs dohs

It's 3:05.
Son las tres y cinco.
sohn lahs trehs ee SEEN-koh

It's 4:10.
Son las cuatro y diez.
sohn lahs KWAH-troh ee dee-EHS

It's 5:15.
Son las cinco y cuarto.
sohn lahs SEEN-koh ee KWAHR-toh

It's 6:20.
Son las seis y veinte.
sohn lahs sehys ee VEHYN-teh

It's 7:25.
Son las siete y veinticinco.
sohn lahs see-EH-teh ee vehyn-tee-SEEN-koh

It's 8:30.
Son las ocho y media.
sohn lahs OH-choh ee MEH-dee-ah

It's 9:35.
Son las diez menos veinticinco.
sohn lahs dee-EHS MEH-nohs-vehyn-tee-SEEN-koh

It's 10:40.
Son las once menos veinte.
sohn lahs OHN-seh MEH-nohs VEHYN-teh

It's 11:45.
Son las doce menos cuarto.
sohn lahs DOH-seh MEH-nohs KWAHR-toh

It's 12:50.
Es la una menos diez.
ehs lah OO-nah MEH-nohs dee-EHS

It's 1:55.
Son las dos menos cinco.
sohn lahs dohs MEH-nohs SEEN-koh

Other Time Phrases

in the morning	*por la mañana*
	pohr lah mah-NYAH-nah
in the afternoon	*por la tarde*
	pohr lah TAHR-deh
in the evening	*por la noche*
	pohr lah NOH-cheh
At what time?	*¿A qué hora?*
	ah keh OH-rah
Since what time?	*¿Desde qué hora?*
	DEHS-deh keh OH-rah
Since two.	*Desde las dos.*
	DEHS-deh lahs dohs
A half-hour ago.	*Hace media hora.*
	AH-seh MEH-dee-ah OH-rah

a second	*un segundo*
	oon seh-GOON-doh
a minute	*un minuto*
	oon mee-NOO-toh
an hour	*una hora*
	OO-nah OH-rah

Days of the Week, Months of the Year

Ah, vacation. Forget your cares, the stress of daily life. Who cares what day of the week it is? Or even what month? Well, it'll come in handy for remembering when you're supposed to get back on that plane.

Days of the Week

day	*día*
	DEE-ah
Sunday	*domingo*
	doh-MEEN-goh
Monday	*lunes*
	LOO-nehs
Tuesday	*martes*
	MAHR-tehs
Wednesday	*miércoles*
	mee-YEHR-koh-lehs
Thursday	*jueves*
	HWEH-vehs
Friday	*viernes*
	vee-YEHR-nehs
Saturday	*sábado*
	SAH-bah-doh

Months of the Year

month	*mes*
	mehs
January	*enero*
	eh-NEH-roh
February	*febrero*
	feh-BREHR-oh
March	*marzo*
	MAHR-soh
April	*abril*
	ah-BREEHL
May	*mayo*
	MAH-yoh
June	*junio*
	HOO-nee-oh
July	*julio*
	HOO-lee-oh
August	*agosto*
	ah-GOHS-toh
September	*septiembre*
	sehp-tee-EHM-breh
October	*octubre*
	ohk-TOO-breh
November	*noviembre*
	noh-vee-EHM-breh
December	*diciembre*
	dee-see-EHM-breh

Seasons

season	*la estación*
	lah eh-stah-see-OHN
winter	*el invierno*
	ehl een-vee-EHR-noh
spring	*la primavera*
	lah pree-mah-VEHR-ah
summer	*el verano*
	ehl vehr-AH-noh
fall	*el otoño*
	ehl oh-TOH-nyoh

 ESSENTIAL

> You're having a lovely visit in Madrid. You've eaten *almuerzo* (lunch) and now it's two in the afternoon and you're ready for some shopping. Well, you may have to wait a few hours. Many shops still close for a few hours in the afternoon for *siesta*.

How's the Weather?

Can't think of anything to say to that friendly-looking person standing next to you in the elevator? No matter the language, there's always that old stand-by: the weather. To talk about the weather you'll use the verbs *hacer*, "to do" or "to make," and *estar*, which is covered in Chapter 1. You'll also use the word *hay*, an adverbial expression that means "there is/are."

HACER: to do, to make

yo hago (AH-goh)
tú haces (AH-sehs)
él, ella, usted hace (AH-seh)
nosotros hacemos (ah-SEH-mohs)
vosotros hacéis (ah-SEYHS)
ellos, ellas, ustedes hacen (AH-sehn)

The literal translations for weather expressions in Spanish are a bit odd to the ear of the English-speaker. The equivalent of "It's cold" is *Hace frío* in Spanish, which literally means "It makes cold."

How's the weather?
¿Qué tiempo hace?
keh tee-EHM-poh AH-seh

It's cold.
Hace frío.
AH-seh FREE-oh

It's cool.
Hace fresco./Está fresco.
AH-seh FREHS-koh/ehs-TAH FREHS-co

It's windy.
Hay viento./Está ventoso.
ahy vee-YEHN-toh/ehs-THA vehn-TOH-soh

It's bad weather.
Hace mal tiempo.
AH-seh mahl tee-EHM-poh

It's hot.
Hace calor.
AH-seh kah-LOHR

It's humid.
Hay humedad.
ahy oo-meh-DAHD

It's sunny.
Hace sol.
AH-seh sohl

It's nice weather.
Hace buen tiempo.
AH-seh bwehn tee-EHM-poh

It's cloudy.
Está nublado.
eh-STAH noo-BLAH-doh

It's raining.
Está lloviendo.
eh-STAH yoh-vee-EHN-doh

There's lightning.
Hay relámpagos.
ahy reh-LAHM-pah-gohs

There's thunder.
Hay truenos.
ahy trew-EH-nohs

It's snowing.
Está nevando.
eh-STAH neh-VAHN-doh

The key to learning any skill is to use it. Now that you know how to talk about the weather, why not get out there and practice what you've learned? In the next chapter, we head to the airport so you can take your Spanish skills out into the world.

 ESSENTIAL

> When talking about the weather in Spanish, remember that like most of the world, Spanish-speaking countries use the metric system, and speak of temperature in terms of degrees Celsius, not Fahrenheit.

Chapter 4
In Transit

You're off to Costa Rica on vacation or maybe to Puerto Rico on a business trip, and you've got your *Everything® Spanish Phrase Book* in hand. This chapter will take you from the plane, to the airport, and on your way, armed with all the Spanish you'll need to make it a great trip.

On the Move with *Ir*

You're certainly excited about your trip, and you will want to talk about where you're going. To do that, you'll need the verb *ir*, "to go." *Ir* is an irregular verb, so you'll have to memorize the present-tense conjugations. Don't let that worry you, though. Just like the verbs *ser* and *estar*, *ir* is used in conversation so often that you'll learn it in no time.

IR: to go
yo voy (voy)
tú vas (vahs)
él, ella, usted va (vah)
nosotros vamos (VAH-mohs)
vosotros vais (vahys)
ellos, ellas, ustedes van (vahn)

Ir is a versatile verb that can be used in several ways. For example, *ir* is the verb you need to indicate your destination:

Voy a Madrid.
I'm going to Madrid.

Sara va al hotel.
Sara goes to the hotel.

Los niños van a la escuela.
The children go to school.

You can also use the verb *ir* to talk about what you're going to do. Just combine the conjugated form of *ir* with the preposition *a* (to) and the infinitive form of another verb, and you've got an easy way to express the future:

Voy a salir a las ocho.
I'm going to leave at eight.

Juan va a leer.
Juan is going to read.

Vamos a caminar juntos.
We are going to walk together.

In Flight

You've got a long flight ahead of you. What better time to try out your language skills? Start up a conversation with the Spanish-speaker in the seat next to you, or chat with the bilingual flight attendant. If you're traveling on a foreign airline, Spanish may very well come in handy if you need to ask a member of the flight crew a question. Refer back to Chapter 3 for a refresher on forming questions in Spanish.

Why has the plane been delayed?
¿Por qué el avión está retrasado?
pohr keh ehl ah-vee-OHN ehs-TAH reh-trah-SAH-doh

Fasten your seatbelt.
Abróchese el cinturón.
ah-BROH-cheh-seh ehl seen-too-ROHN

My seatbelt won't fasten.
Mi cinturón no abrocha.
mee seen-too-ROHN noh ah-BROH-chah

May I have a blanket?
¿Puedo tener una manta?
PWEH-doh teh-NEHR OO-nah MAHN-tah

I'd like a vegetarian meal.
Quisiera una comida vegetariana.
kee-see-EHR-ah OOH-nah koh-MEE-dah veh-heh-tah-ree-AH-nah

What time are we going to land?
¿A qué hora vamos a aterrizar?
ah keh OH-rah VAH-mos ah ah-teh-rree-SAHR

May I change my seat?
¿Puedo cambiar mi asiento?
PWEH-doh kahm-bee-AHR mee ah-see-EHN-toh

I'd like an aisle seat.
Quisiera un asiento junto al pasillo.
kee-see-EHR-ah oon ah-see-EHN-toh HOON-toh ahl pah-SEE-yoh

I'd like a window seat.
Quisiera un asiento junto a la ventana.
kee-see-EHR-ah oon ah-see-EHN-toh HOON-toh ah lah
vehn-TAH-nah

Will there be a movie shown?
¿Va a haber una película?
vah a ah-BEHR OO-nah peh-LEE-koo-lah

 ALERT!

When traveling, keep in mind that the phrase
for emergency exit is *la salida de emergencia.*
If you need emergency help, you need to ask
for *socorro.*

What movie are we going to see?
¿Cuál película vamos a ver?
kwahl peh-LEE-koo-lah VAH-mohs ah vehr

May I have some water?
¿Puedo tener un poco de agua?
PWEH-doh TEH-nehr oon POH-koh deh AH-gwah

In-Flight Vocabulary

emergency exit	*la salida de emergencia*
	lah sah-LEE-dah deh eh-mehr-HEN-see-ah
life vest	*el chaleco salvavidas*
	ehl chah-LEH-koh sahl-vah-VEE-dahs
airplane	*el avión*
	ehl ah-vee-OHN
pilot	*el piloto, la pilota*
	ehl pee-LOH-toh/lah pee-LOH-tah
altitude	*la altitud*
	lah ahl-tee-TOOD
baggage	*el portaequipajes*
compartment	ehl pohr-tah-eh-kee-PAH-hehs
row	*la fila*
	lah FEE-lah
seat	*el asiento*
	ehl ah-see-EHN-toh
pillow	*la almohada*
	lah ahl-moh-AH-dah
take-off	*el despegue*
	ehl dehs-PEH-geh
landing	*el aterrizaje*
	ehl ah-teh-rree-SAH-heh
headphones	*los auriculares*
	lohs ow-ree-koo-LAH-rehs
flight attendant	*el/la azafato/a*
	ehl/lah ah-sah-FAH-toh/tah
boarding card	*el pase de abordar*
	ehl PAH-seh deh ah-bohr-DAHR

| carry-on luggage | *equipaje de mano* |
| | eh-kee-PAH-heh deh MAH-noh |

Navigating the Airport

You've arrived! Now let's get you through the airport, past customs, and on your way.

Airport Vocabulary

arrival	*la llegada*
	lah yeh-GAH-dah
baggage	*el equipaje*
	ehl eh-kee-PAH-heh
baggage claim	*reclamación de equipajes*
	reh-klah-mah-see-OHN deh eh-kee-PAH-hehs
boarding gate	*la puerta de embarque*
	lah PWEHR-tah deh ehm-BAHR-keh
bus stop	*la parada de autobús*
	lah pah-RAH-dah deh ow-toh-BOOS
car rental	*el alquiler de coches*
	ehl ahl-kee-LEHR deh KOH-chehs
cart	*el carrito*
	ehl kah-RREE-toh
departure	*la salida*
	lah sah-LEE-dah
elevator	*los ascensores*
	lohs ah-sehn-SOHR-ehs
entrance	*la entrada*
	lah ehn-TRAH-dah

Airport Vocabulary (continued)

exit	*la salida*
	lah sah-LEE-dah
flight	*el vuelo*
	ehl VWEH-loh
to miss the flight	*perder el vuelo*
	pehr-DEHR ehl VWEH-loh
money exchange	*el cambio de dinero*
	ehl CAHM-bee-oh deh dee-NEH-roh
lost baggage	*el equipaje extraviado*
	ehl eh-kee-PAH-heh ehks-trah-vee-AH-doh
lost and found	*la oficina de objetos perdidos*
	lah oh-fee-SEE-nah deh ohb-HEH-tohs pehr-DEE-dohs
moving walkway	*las cintas transportadoras*
	lahs SEEN-tahs trahns-pohr-tah-DOHR-ahs
restrooms	*los baños*
	lohs BAHN-yohs
ticket	*el boleto*
	ehl boh-LEH-toh
hallway	*el pasillo*
	ehl pah-SEE-yoh

Declaring Your Belongings

The verb *tener*, "to have" will come in handy as you pass through customs. Use it to express what you have or don't have with you.

TENER: to have

yo tengo (TEHN-goh)
tú tienes (tee-EHN-ehs)
él, ella, usted tiene (tee-EHN-eh)
nosotros tenemos (teh-NEH-mohs)
vosotros tenéis (tehn-EHYS)
ellos, ellas, ustedes tienen (tee-EHN-ehn)

Tener is used in Spanish in the same way we use the verb "to have" in English:

Tengo dos hijos.
I have two children.

Carla tiene una visa estudiantil.
Clara has a student visa.

Tenemos familia aquí.
We have family here.

Just as in English, the verb *tener* can be used in the expression "to have to (do something)." In Spanish, the phrase is *tener que* + infinitive:

Tengo que salir ahora.
I have to leave now.

Marco tiene que comer sus vegetales.
Marco has to eat his vegetables.

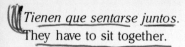

Tienen que sentarse juntos.
They have to sit together.

Customs Vocabulary

customs	*la aduana*
	lah ah-DWAH-nah
duty free	*libre de impuestos*
	LEE-breh deh eem-PWEH-stohs
flight number	*el número de vuelo*
	ehl NOO-meh-roh deh VWEH-lo
form of identification	*la forma de identificación*
	lah FOHR-mah deh ee-dehn-tee-fee-kah-see-OHN
passport	*el pasaporte*
	ehl pah-sah-POHR-teh

In addition to the vocabulary, here are some questions and phrases for going through the customs:

Here is my passport.
Aquí está mi pasaporte.
ah-KEE eh-STAH mee pah-sah-POHR-teh

Do you have anything to declare?
¿Tiene algo que declarar?
tee-EHN-eh AHL-goh keh deh-klahr-AHR

Yes, I have something to declare.
Sí, tengo algo que declarar.
see TEHN-goh AHL-goh keh deh-klahr-AHR

I have nothing to declare.
No tengo nada que declarar.
noh TEHN-goh NAH-dah keh deh-klahr-AHR

I'm here on business.
Estoy aquí de negocios.
eh-STOY ah-KEE deh neh-GOH-see-ohs

I'm here on vacation.
Estoy aquí de vacaciones.
eh-STOY ah-KEE deh vah-kah-see-OH-nehs

I'll be here for two weeks.
Estaré aquí dos semanas.
eh-stahr-EH ah-KEE dohs seh-MAH-nahs

I'm going to stay at the Hotel Gran Vía.
Me voy a quedar en el Hotel Gran Vía.
meh voy ah keh-DAHR ehn ehl oh-TEHL grahn VEE-ah

 ESSENTIAL

Flight attendants on international flights to and
from Spanish-speaking countries usually speak
Spanish as well as English. What a great opportunity to practice your new language skills!

Chapter 5
At the Hotel

Your hotel room is your home away from home. If you know how to ask for what you need, your stay will be that much more pleasant. This chapter will help ensure you have all the comforts of home while traveling abroad.

Tengo — I have to P. 61

Checking In, Checking Out

You've made it from the airport to the hotel front desk. And you've been using your Spanish all the way, thanks to this book, haven't you? Now, let's get you checked in. Courtesy is extremely important in many Spanish-speaking cultures. Remember to say *por favor* (please) and *gracias* (thank you), and you'll get much better service. And as always, when in doubt, use the formal you, *usted*.

I have a reservation.
Tengo una reservación.
TEHN-goh OO-nah rehs-ehr-vah-see-OHN

I don't have a reservation.
No tengo reservación.
noh TEHN-goh rehs-ehr-vah-see-OHN

I'll be staying for three nights.
Me voy a quedar tres noches.
meh voy ah keh-DAHR trehs NOH-chehs

We'd like a double bed.
Quisiéramos una cama matrimonial.
kee-see-EHR-ah-mohs OO-nah KAH-mah
mah-tree-moh-nee-AHL

We'd like a room with a private bath.
Quisiéramos un cuarto con baño privado.
kee-see-EHR-ah-mohs oon KWAHR-toh kohn BAH-nyoh
pree-VAH-doh

What floor is the gym on?
¿En qué piso está el gimnasio?
ehn keh PEE-soh eh-STAH ehl heem-NAH-see-oh

Please give me a wake-up call at 7 A.M.
Por favor, llame para despertarme a las siete de la mañana.
pohr fah-VOHR, YAH-meh PAH-rah dehs-pehr-TAHR-meh ah lahs see-EH-teh deh lah mah-NYAH-nah

How do you make an outside call?
¿Cómo se marca para la calle?
KOH-moh seh MAHR-kah PAH-rah lah CAH-yeh

Our room hasn't been cleaned.
No han limpiado nuestro cuarto.
noh ahn leem-pee-AH-doh noo-EHS-troh KWAHR-toh

The bill is incorrect.
La cuenta no está correcta.
lah KWEHN-tah noh eh-STAH koh-REHK-tah

I'm ready to check out.
Estoy listo/a para desocupar.
eh-STOY LEE-stoh/stah PAH-rah dehs-oh-koo-PAHR

Can I have the bill, please?
¿Puedo tener la cuenta, por favor?
PWEH-doh teh-NEHR lah KWEHN-tah pohr fah-VOHR

Hotel Vocabulary

air-conditioning	*el aire acondicionado*
	ehl AY-reh ah-kohn-dee-see-oh-NAH-doh
bar	*el bar*
	ehl bahr
bathroom	*el cuarto de baño*
	ehl KWAHR-toh deh BAH-nyoh
bathtub	*la bañera*
	lah bah-NYEH-rah
bed	*la cama*
	lah KAH-mah
double bed	*la cama matrimonial*
	lah KAH-mah mah-tree-moh-nee-AHL
twin bed	*la cama individual*
	lah KAH-mah een-dee-vee-doo-AHL
bill	*la cuenta*
	lah KWEHN-tah
doorman	*el portero*
	ehl pohr-TEH-roh
elevator	*el ascensor*
	ehl ah-sehn-SOHR
floor	*el piso*
	ehl PEE-soh
gym	*el gimnasio*
	ehl heem-NAH-see-oh
hairdryer	*el secador de pelo*
	ehl seh-kah-DOHR deh PEH-loh
hanger	*la percha*
	lah PEHR-chah

hostel	*el hostal*
	ehl ohs-STAHL
hotel	*el hotel*
	ehl oh-TEHL
ice cubes	*los cubitos de hielo*
	lohs koo-BEE-tohs deh ee-YEHL-oh
key	*la llave*
	lah YAH-beh
lamp	*la lámpara*
	lah LAHM-pah-rah
light	*la luz*
	lah loos
manager	*el/la gerente*
	ehl/lah heh-REHN-teh
pillow	*la almohada*
	lah ahl-moh-AH-dah
reservation	*la reservación*
	lah rehs-ehr-bah-see-OHN
room	*la habitación*
	lah ah-bee-tah-see-OHN
safe (box)	*la caja de seguridad*
	lah KAH-hah deh seh-goo-ree-DAHD
shampoo	*el champú*
	ehl chahm-POO
sheet	*la sábana*
	lah SAH-bah-nah
shower	*la ducha*
	lah DOO-chah
swimming pool	*la piscina*
	lah pee-SEE-nah

Hotel Vocabulary (continued) *Note: accent where*
The / accent
is.

telephone	*el teléfono*
	ehl teh-LEH-foh-noh
television	*la televisión*
	lah teh-leh-bee-see-OHN
toilet	*el water, el inodoro*
	ehl WAH-tehr, ehl ee-noh-DOH-roh
toilet paper	*el papel higiénico*
	ehl pah-PEHL ee-HYEHN-ee-koh
towel	*la toalla*
	lah toh-AY-yah
bath towel	*la toalla de baño*
	lah toh-AY-yah deh BAH-nyoh
face towel	*la toalla para la cara*
	lah toh-AY-yah PAH-rah lah KAH-rah
hand towel	*la toalla para las manos*
	lah toh-AY-yah PAH-rah lahs MAH-nohs
sink	*el lavabo*
	ehl lah-VAH-boh
water	*el agua*
	ehl AH-gooah
cold water	*el agua fría*
	ehl AH-gooah FREE-ah
hot water	*el agua caliente*
	ehl AH-gooah kah-lee-EHN-teh
window	*la ventana*
	lah vehn-TAH-nah

Running Errands

After a delicious lunch in Oaxaca, you realize more *mole* landed on your suit than in your mouth. You catch your reflection in the pond in el *Parque Retiro* in Madrid and notice that it's been WAY too long since your last haircut. Climbing into a *chivo* in Cartagena, your boot heel catches on the stair and snaps right off. You need some professional help.

 ESSENTIAL

> Little gestures of courtesy really do make a difference. When asking for something you want, it's better to use *quisiera*, "I would like," rather than *quiero*, "I want."

What time do you open?
¿A qué hora abre usted?
ah keh OH-rah AH-breh OO-stehd

What time do you close?
¿A qué hora cierra usted?
ah keh OH-rah see-YEHRR-ah OO-stehd

Are you open on Sundays?
¿Está abierto los domingos?
eh-STAH ah-bee-YEHR-toh lohs doh-MEEN-gohs

Can you help me, please?
¿Puede usted ayudarme, por favor?
PWEH-deh OO-stehd ah-yoo-DAHR-meh pohr fah-VOHR

How much do I owe you?
¿Cuánto le debo?
KWAHN-toh leh DEH-boh

Can I pay with a credit card?
¿Puedo pagar con tarjeta de crédito?
PWEH-doh pah-GAHR kohn tahr-HEH-tah deh KREH-dee-toh

Can I pay with traveler's checks?
¿Puedo pagar con cheques de viajero?
PWEH-doh pah-GAHR kohn CHEH-kehs deh bee-ah-HEHR-oh

May I have a receipt?
¿Me puede dar el recibo?
meh PWEH-deh dahr ehl reh-SEE-boh

Could you please . . . ?
¿Podría usted . . . , por favor?
poh-DREE-ah OO-stehd . . . , pohr fah-VOHR

Is the tip included?
¿Está incluida la propina?
eh-STAH een-kloo-EE-dah lah proh-PEE-nah

Could you give me . . . ?
¿Podría darme . . . ?
poh-DREE-ah DAHR-meh

Can you deliver it to my hotel?
¿Puede enviarlo a mi hotel?
PWEH-deh ehn-vee-AHR-loh ah mee oh-TEHL

 ALERT!

> If you're sending your laundry out to be cleaned in a Spanish-speaking country, make sure the care labels in your clothing have either Spanish instructions or international symbols. Otherwise, your favorite sweater might come back just the right size for your five-year-old niece.

If You Packed Light

Maybe you like to pack light and get your clothes laundered or dry cleaned when you're away. Or maybe you'll be away longer than just a few weeks. Here are the words and phrases you'll need if you plan to visit the local dry cleaner or laundromat:

Can you please dry clean this for me?
¿Puede usted limpiar esto en seco, por favor?
PWEH-deh OO-stehd leehm-PEEAHR-meh EH-stoh ehn SEH-koh pohr fah-VOHR

Can you press this for me, please?
¿Puede usted plancharme esto, por favor?
PWEH-deh OO-stehd plahn-CHAHR-meh EH-stoh pohr
fah-VOHR

Can you repair this for me, please?
¿Puede usted remendarme esto, por favor?
PWEH-deh OO-stehd reh-mehn-DAHR-meh EH-stoh pohr
fah-VOHR

There is a stain here.
Hay una mancha aquí.
ahy OO-nah MAHN-chah ah-KEE

Is this machine taken?
¿Está ocupada esta máquina?
eh-STAH oh-koo-PAH-dah EHS-tah MAH-kee-nah

How does this machine work?
¿Cómo funciona esta máquina?
KOH-moh foonk-see-YOH-nah EHS-tah MAH-kee-nah

This machine is broken.
Esta máquina no funciona.
EHS-tah MAH-kee-nah noh foonk-see-YOH-nah

Where can I buy detergent?
¿Dónde puedo comprar detergente?
DOHN-deh PWEH-doh kohm-PRAHR deh-tehr-HEN-teh

At the Dry Cleaner's

dry cleaner's	*la tintorería*
	lah teen-toh-rehr-EE-ah
a hole	*un hueco*
	oon WEH-koh
a tear	*un rasgón*
	oon RAHS-gohn
a missing button	*un botón perdido*
	oon boh-TOHN pehr-DEE-doh
a broken zipper	*una cremallera rota*
	OO-nah creh-mah-YEHR-ah ROH-tah
a stain	*una mancha*
	OO-nah MAHN-chah
I need it . . .	*Lo/la necesito . . .*
	loh/lah neh-seh-SEE-toh
I need them . . .	*Los/las necesito . . .*
	lohs/lahs neh-seh-SEE-toh
today	*hoy*
	oy
tomorrow	*mañana*
	mah-NYAH-nah
in an hour	*en una hora*
	ehn OO-nah OH-rah
this afternoon	*esta tarde*
	EH-stah TAHR-deh
tonight	*esta noche*
	EH-stah NOH-cheh
tomorrow morning	*mañana por la mañana*
	mah-NYAH-nah pohr lah mah-NYAH-nah

At the Laundromat

bleach	*lejía*	
	leh-HEE-ah	
clothing	*ropa*	
	ROH-pah	
clothes dryer	*secadora*	
	seh-kah-DOHR-ah	
detergent	*detergente*	
	deh-tehr-HEN-teh	
laundromat	*lavandería*	
	lah-vahn-dehr-EE-ah	
washing machine	*lavadora*	
	lah-vah-DOHR-ah	

 FACT

Unlike English, the days of the week and months of the year are not capitalized in Spanish.

At the Hair Salon/Barber Shop

just a trim	*solo un recorte*	
	SOH-loh oon reh-KOHR-teh	
Please shave my . . .	*Por favor, aféiteme . . .*	
	pohr fah-VOHR ah-FEY-teh-meh	
beard	*la barba*	
	lah BAHR-bah	
mustache	*el bigote*	
	ehl bee-GOH-teh	

sideburns	*las patillas*
	lahs pah-TEE-yahs
barbershop	*la barbería*
	lah bahr-beh-REE-ah
beauty salon	*el salón de belleza*
	ehl sah-LOHN deh beh-YEH-sah
blow dry	*secar el pelo*
	seh-KAHR ehl PEH-loh
bangs	*el flequillo*
	ehl fleh-KEE-yoh
to comb	*peinar*
	pey-NAHR
curly	*rizado*
	ree-SAH-doh
hair	*el pelo*
	ehl PEH-loh
a haircut	*un corte de pelo*
	oon KOHR-teh deh PEH-loh
hairstyle	*peinado*
	pey-NAH-doh
highlights	*reflejos*
	reh-FLEH-hohs
long	*largo*
	LAHR-goh
short	*corto*
	KOHR-toh
a manicure	*una manicura*
	OO-nah mah-nee-KOO-rah
a pedicure	*una pedicura*
	OO-nah peh-dee-KOO-rah

At the Hair Salon/Barber Shop (continued)

a perm	*una permanente*
	OO-nah pehr-mah-NEHN-teh
to shave	*afeitarse*
	ah-fey-TAHR-seh
wavy	*ondulado*
	ohn-doo-LAH-doh
a waxing	*una depilación*
	oo-nah deh-pee-lah-see-OHN

From Head to Toe

Whether you need a haircut, or your favorite pair of boots just lost a heel while you were touring the local sites, here are the phrases that will help you take care of the problem.

At the Shoe Repair Shop

arch	*el empeine*
	ehl ehm-PEY-neh
boot	*la bota*
	lah BOH-tah
broken	*roto/a*
	ROH-toh/tah
heel	*el tacón*
	ehl tah-KOHN
scuff	*la raya*
	lah RAH-yah
shoe	*el zapato*
	ehl sah-PAH-toh

shoelace	*el cordón de zapato*
	ehl kohr-DOHN deh sah-PAH-toh
sole	*la suela*
	lah SWEH-lah

I need a shoe shine.
Necesito una limpieza de zapatos.
neh-seh-SEE-toh OO-nah leem-pee-YEH-sah deh sah-PAH-tohs

Can you repair this . . . for me?
¿Puede usted remendarme este/a . . . ?
PWEH-deh OO-stehd reh-mehn-DAHR-meh EH-steh/ah

At the Camera Shop

battery	*la pila*
	lah PEE-lah
camera	*la cámara*
	lah KAH-mah-rah
camera film	*la película*
	lah peh-LEE-koo-lah
exposures	*las exposiciones*
	lahs ehs-poh-see-see-YOHN-ehs
video camera	*la cámara de video*
	lah KAH-mah-rah deh vee-DEH-oh

Can you repair this camera?
¿Puede usted reparar esta cámara?
PWEH-deh OO-stehd reh-pah-RAHR EH-stah KAH-mah-rah

Do you have film for this camera?
¿Tiene usted película para esta cámara?
tee-EHN-eh OO-stehd peh-LEE-koo-lah PAH-rah EH-steh
KAH-mah-rah

I'd like to have this film developed.
Quisiera que me revele este rollo.
kee-see-YEHR-ah keh meh reh-VEH-leh EH-steh ROY-oh

You're all settled, with everything you need in your
comfortable hotel room, and you even have a new
haircut! Time to get out there and see the sights. Next
we'll talk about getting around town, reading signs, and
asking directions.

 QUESTION?

**What do you say when you want to get
someone's attention? And what about
when you want to get past someone who's
blocking your way?**
In English, "excuse me" would work in both
these cases. In Spanish, there are two separate
phrases. To get someone's attention, say *dis-
culpe* (dees-COOL-peh). To get around someone,
you can use *con permiso* (cohn pehr-MEE-soh).

Chapter 6
On the Move

Making your way around a strange city can be daunting, especially if you don't speak the language. Which metro line takes you to the museum? Do you have to transfer buses to get from your hotel to the embassy? How much are train tickets for that excursion to the neighboring town? If you get lost, how do you ask for directions? This chapter covers what you need to know to navigate on foot or by car, subway, bus, or train.

Getting Around

For coming, going, traveling, and wandering, you'll need to add some new verbs of motion to your arsenal:

- *andar:* to walk
- *caminar:* to walk
- *conducir:* to drive
- *tomar:* to take
- *viajar:* to travel

ANDAR: to walk

yo ando (AHN-do)
tú andas (AHN-dahs)
él, ella, usted anda (AHN-dah)
nosotros andamos (ahn-DAH-mohs)
vosotros andáis (ahn-DAHYS)
ellos, ellas, ustedes andan (AHN-dahn)

Here are a few examples of how you might use the verb *andar:*

Yo ando al museo.
I walk to the museum.

Carla y yo andamos juntos.
Carla and I walk together.

Las niñas andan en bicicleta.
The girls ride bicycles.

Caught you off guard with that last example? *Andar* is most often translated as "to walk," but this verb can also be used to mean "to go" or "to ride." Don't worry! The context it's used in will pretty much always make the meaning perfectly clear.

 FACT

> Spanish words for forms of transportation are very easy to remember, because most of them are cognates. For example, a taxi is *un taxi* in Spanish. A bus is *un autobús*. A train is *un tren*. Get the idea?

CAMINAR: to walk

yo camino (kah-MEE-noh)
tú caminas (kah-MEE-nahs)
él, ella, usted camina (kah-MEE-nah)
nosotros caminamos (kah-mee-NAH-mohs)
vosotros camináis (kah-mee-NAYHS)
ellos, ellas, ustedes caminan (kah-MEE-nahn)

The verb *caminar* is a synonym of *andar*. Here are a few examples of how it might be used:

En Miami caminamos por la playa.
We walk on the beach in Miami.

¿Vosotros camináis en la Plaza Mayor cada día?
Do you walk in the Plaza Mayor every day?

Yo prefiero caminar por la tarde.
I prefer walking in the afternoon.

In the last example, the first-person form of *preferir*
(to prefer) was combined with the infinitive form of *cam-*
inar—a simple way to express more complex thoughts.

CONDUCIR: to drive

yo conduzco (kohn-DOOS-koh)
tú conduces (kohn-DOO-sehs)
él, ella, usted conduce (kohn-DOO-seh)
nosotros conducimos (kohn-doo-SEE-mohs)
vosotros conducís (kohn-doo-SEES)
ellos, ellas, ustedes conducen (kohn-DOO-sehn)

Use *conducir* to refer to driving a vehicle:

Tú conduces muy bien.
You drive very well.

Es difícil conducir en una cuidad nueva.
It's difficult to drive in a new city.

Linda y Julio conducen un coche verde.
Linda and Julio drive a green car.

TOMAR: to take

yo tomo (TOH-moh)
tú tomas (TOH-mahs)
él, ella, usted toma (TOH-mah)
nosotros tomamos (toh-MAH-mohs)
vosotros tomáis (toh-MAHYS)
ellos, ellas, ustedes toman (TOH-mahn)

 ESSENTIAL

Two phrases the traveler should never be without: I'm lost, *estoy perdido/a* (eh-STOY pehr-DEE-doh/ah). Can you help me? *¿Puede ayudarme?* (PWEH-deh ah-yoo-DAHR-meh).

The verb *tomar* may be used to mean "take" in the sense of taking something, or it may indicate the "taking" of food or drink (it's used more frequently to mean "to drink"):

Tome el dinero.
Take the money.

Tomamos un taxi al restaurante.
We take a taxi to the restaurant.

Yo nunca tomo agua fría.
I never drink cold water.

To say someone is "tomado" is to say they're drunk. If someone says, "Yo no tomo" they are telling you they don't drink alcohol.

VIAJAR: to travel

yo viajo (vee-YAH-hoh)
tú viajas (vee-YAH-hahs)
él, ella, usted viaja (vee-YAH-hah)
nosotros viajamos (vee-yah-HAH-mohs)
vosotros viajáis (vee-yah-HAHYS)
ellos, ellas, ustedes viajan (vee-YAH-hahn)

The use of *viajar* is straightforward:

Ellos viajan juntos a España.
They travel to Spain together.

¿Cúando vas a viajar conmigo?
When are you going to travel with me?

Ella no viaja nunca.
She never travels.

Where Am I?

Finding your way is a lot easier if you know how to ask for directions. It's even easier if you understand the response!

Where is . . . ?
¿Dónde está . . . ?
DOHN-deh eh-STAH

I'm going to . . .
Voy a . . .
vohy ah . . .

How do I get to . . . from here?
¿Cómo voy a . . . de aquí?
KOH-moh vohy ah . . . deh ah-KEE

Can you help me?
¿Puede ayudarme?
PWEH-deh ah-yoo-DAHR-meh

Is it far?
¿Es lejos?
eh LEH-hohs

Can I walk from here to there?
¿Puedo caminar de aquí hasta allá?
PWEH-doh kah-mee-NAHR deh ah-KEE AH-stah ah-YAH

Where is the nearest bus stop?
¿Dónde está la parada de autobús más cercana?
DOHN-de eh-STAH lah pah-RAH-dah deh ow-toh-BOOS
mahs sehr-KAH-nah

Where can I buy a ticket?
¿Dónde puedo comprar un billete?
DOHN-de PWEH-doh kohm-PRAHR oon bee-YEH-teh

Can you show it to me on this map?
¿Puede enseñármelo en esta mapa?
PWEH-deh ehn-sehn-YAHR-meh-loh ehn EH-stah MAH-pah

Locations

American Embassy	*la embajada americana*
	lah ehm-bah-HAH-dah ah-meh-ree-KAH-nah
metro station	*la estación de metro*
	lah ehs-tah-see-OHN deh MEH-troh
train station	*la estación de trenes*
	lah ehs-tah-see-OHN deh TREHN-ehs
block	*la manzana*
	mahn-SAH-nah
building	*el edificio*
	ehl eh-dee-FEE-see-yoh
sidewalk	*la acera*
	lah ah-SEH-rah
street	*la calle*
	lah KAH-yeh
street corner	*la esquina*
	lah eh-SKEE-nah

Prepositions of Location

across from	*en frente a*
	ehn FREHN-teh ah
ahead	*más adelante*
	mahs ah-deh-LAHN-teh
behind	*detrás de*
	deh-TRAHS deh
near	*cerca*
	SEHR-kah
next to	*al lado de*
	ahl LAH-doh deh
far	*lejos*
	LEH-hos

Directions

east	*este*
	EHS-teh
left	*izquierda*
	eehs-kee-EHR-dah
north	*norte*
	NOHR-teh
right	*derecha*
	deh-REH-chah
south	*sur*
	soor
straight	*derecho*
	deh-REH-choh
west	*oeste*
	oh-EHS-teh

A Few Verbs of Command

continue	*siga*
	SEE-gah
take	*tome*
	TOH-meh
turn	*doble*
	DOH-bleh
walk	*camine*
	kah-MEE-neh
cross	*cruce*
	KROO-seh
go back	*vuelva*
	VWEHL-vah
go down	*baje*
	BAH-heh
go past	*pase*
	PAH-seh
go up	*suba*
	SOO-bah

Means of Transportation

If the distance from Point A to Point B is farther than your feet can carry you, you'll need to hop on one form of transportation or another. Here are the phrases and terms you'll need to get you where you're going.

How much is the fare?
¿Cuánto es la tarifa?
KWAHN-toh ehs lah tah-REE-fah

Is this seat taken?
¿Está ocupado este asiento?
eh-STAH oh-koo-PAH-doh EH-steh ah-see-EHN-toh

How many stops before . . . ?
¿Cuántas paradas hasta . . . ?
KWAHN-tahs pah-RAH-dahs AH-stah

What is the next stop?
¿Cuál es la próxima parada?
kwahl ehs lah PROHK-see-mah pah-RAH-dah

Excuse me. I'm getting off here.
Con permiso. Bajo aquí.
kohn pehr-MEE-soh BAH-hoh ah-KEE

Take a Cab

fare	*el precio del viaje*
	ehl PREH-see-oh dehl vee-AH-heh
taxi	*el taxi*
	ehl TAHK-see
taxi driver	*el taxista*
	ehl tahk-SEES-tah
taxi stand	*la parada de taxis*
	lah pah-RAH-dah deh TAHK-sees
tip	*la propina*
	lah proh-PEE-nah

Here are a few additional phrases for communicating with cabbies:

Stop here.
Pare aquí.
PAH-reh ah-KEE

Please wait for me.
Espéreme, por favor.
ehs-PEH-reh-meh pohr fah-VOHR

Can you please open the trunk?
¿Puede abrir el maletero, por favor?
PWEH-deh ah-BREEHR ehl mah-leh-TEH-roh pohr fah-VOHR

How much do I owe you?
¿Cuánto le debo?
KWAHN-toh leh DEH-boh

Ride the Subway

subway	*el metro*
	ehl MEH-troh
ticket machine	*la máquina de billetes*
	lah MAH-kee-nah deh bee-YEH-tehs
fare	*la tarifa*
	lah tah-REE-fah
metro station	*la estación de metro*
	lah eh-stah-see-YOHN deh MEH-troh
platform	*el andén*
	ehl ahn-DEHN

Can I connect to the . . . line here?
¿Puedo cambiar a la línea . . . aquí?
PWEH-doh kahm-bee-YAHR ah lah LEE-nay-ah . . . ah-KEE

Which line goes to . . . ?
¿Cuál línea va a . . . ?
kwahl LEE-nay-ah vah ah

Take the Bus

bus	*el autobús*
	ehl ow-toh-BOOS
bus driver	*el conductor*
	ehl kohn-dook-TOHR
fare	*la tarifa*
	lah tah-REE-fah
bus stop	*la parada de autobús*
	lah pah-RAH-dah deh ow-toh-BOOS
bus station	*la estación de autobús*
	lah eh-stah-see-OHN deh ow-toh-BOOS
ticket	*el billete*
	ehl bee-YEH-teh

In the Train

train station	*la estación de trenes*
	lah eh-stah-see-OHN deh trehn-ehs
schedule	*el horario*
	ehl oh-RAH-ree-oh
conductor	*el cobrador*
	ehl koh-brah-DOHR

In the Train (continued)

first class ticket	*el billete de primera clase*
	ehl bee-YEH-teh deh pree-MEH-rah KLAH-seh
second class ticket	*el billete de segunda clase*
	ehl bee-YEH-teh deh seh-GOON-dah KLAH-seh
smoking compartment	*el compartimiento para fumadores*
	ehl com-pahr-tee-mee-EHN-toh PAH-rah foo-mah-DOHR-ehs
non-smoking compartment	*el compartimiento para no fumadores*
	ehl com-pahr-tee-mee-EHN-toh PAH-rah noh foo-mah-DOHR-ehs
sleeper compartment	*el compartimiento con literas*
	ehl com-pahr-tee-mee-EHN-toh kohn lee-TEH-rahs
platform	*el andén*
	ehl ahn-DEHN
ticket	*el billete*
	ehl bee-YEH-teh
ticket window	*la taquilla*
	lah tah-KEE-yah
one-way ticket	*el billete sencillo*
	ehl bee-YEH-teh sehn-SEE-yoh
round-trip ticket	*el billete de ida y vuelta*
	ehl bee-YEH-teh deh EE-dah ee VWEHL-tah

Renting a Car

car	*el coche*
	ehl KOH-cheh
to rent	*alquilar*
	ahl-kee-LAHR
car rental	*el alquiler de coches*
	ehl ahl-kee-LEHR deh KOH-chehs
driver's license	*el carné de conducir*
	ehl kahr-NEH deh kohn-doo-SEER
breakdown	*la avería*
	lah ah-veh-REE-ah
car accident	*el choque*
	ehl CHOH-keh
traffic	*el tráfico*
	ehl TRAH-fee-koh
dent	*la abolladura*
	lah ah-boh-yah-DOO-rah
gasoline	*la gasolina*
	lah gah-soh-LEE-nah
excess kilometers	*los kilómetros de exceso*
	lohs kee-LOH-meh-trohs deh ehk-SEHS-oh
oil	*el aceite*
	ehl ah-SAY-teh
directions	*las señas*
	lahs SEH-nyahs
insurance	*el seguro*
	ehl seh-GOO-roh
highway	*la carretera*
	lah kah-reh-TEH-rah

Renting a Car (continued)

street	*la calle*
	lah KAH-yeh
toll	*el peaje*
	ehl peh-AH-heh
bridge	*el puente*
	ehl PWEHN-teh

With all this traipsing about town, you've probably worked up quite a hunger. In the next chapter you'll learn food vocabulary words so you can find what you want (and maybe, more importantly, what you *don't* want) on a menu. We wouldn't want you to end up with a tortilla made with pigs' brains (yes, you can really get that in Spain) unless that's what you meant to order.

 ALERT!

It won't help you to ask for directions if you can't understand the response. If you ask for help and the response is spoken too quickly for you to understand, you can say *¿Puede hablar más despacio, por favor?* (PWEH-deh ah-BLAHR mahs dehs-PAH-see-oh pohr fah-VOHR) Can you please speak more slowly?

Chapter 7
Dining Options

For many people, one of the most enjoyable parts of exploring a new culture and language is getting to taste new foods. For others, it's more about the people, or the architecture, or the art. Regardless of how you approach it, though, you've got to eat. And you'll probably want to know what it is you're eating. Are you a vegetarian, for example? If so, you'll certainly want to learn the vocabulary words for types of meat, so you know what NOT to order!

Eating and Drinking

You'll find the following set of verbs especially helpful when ordering in a restaurant, shopping in a grocery store, or just talking about your culinary likes and dislikes:

* *comer*: to eat
* *beber*: to drink
* *querer*: to want
* *necesitar*: to need
* *gustar*: to like, to be pleasing to

And don't forget about *tomar* (Chapter 6), which means "to take" but is also used to mean "to drink" and, less often, "to eat."

COMER: to eat

yo como (KOH-moh)
tú comes (KOH-mehs)
él, ella, usted come (KOH-meh)
nosotros comemos (koh-MEH-mohs)
vosotros coméis (koh-MEHYS)
ellos, ellas, ustedes comen (KOH-mehn)

Armed with the verb *comer,* you can tell the waiter that you don't eat certain foods, or use it in any number of situations:

Yo no como carne.
I don't eat meat.

Juan Carlos siempre come almuerzo.
Juan Carlos always eats lunch.

Ustedes comen demasiado.
You eat too much.

BEBER: to drink

yo bebo (BEH-boh)
tú bebes (BEH-behs)
él, ella, usted bebe (BEH-beh)
nosotros bebemos (beh-BEH-mohs)
vosotros bebéis (beh-BEHYS)
ellos, ellas, ustedes beben (BEH-behn)

Beber is used to talk about drinking, although sometimes *tomar* is used instead:

La niña bebe leche.
The girl drinks milk.

¿Por qué bebes tanto café?
Why do you drink so much coffee?

Ellos beben gaseosa cuando comen pizza.
They drink soda when they eat pizza.

Billy toma su té en el patio.
Billy drinks his tea on the patio.

QUERER: to want

yo quiero (kee-YEHR-oh)
tú quieres (kee-YEHR-ehs)
él, ella, usted quiere (kee-YEHR-eh)
nosotros queremos (keh-REH-mohs)
vosotros queréis (keh-REHYS)
ellos, ellas, ustedes quieren (kee-YEHR-ehn)

In Spanish, the verb *querer* is used to mean "want" in the sense of liking or needing something:

¿Qué queréis comer?
What would you like to eat?

¿Quieres más agua?
Do you want more water?

No quiero pimienta.
I don't want pepper.

Also note that to ask for what you would like, you need to use the imperfect subjunctive form of *querer:*

QUERER in Imperfect Subjunctive

yo quisiera (kee-see-EHR-ah)
tú quisieras (kee-see-EHR-ahs)
él, ella, usted quisiera (kee-see-EHR-ah)
nosotros quisiéramos (kee-see-EHR-ah-mohs)
vosotros quisierais (kee-see-EHR-ahys)
ellos, ellas, ustedes quisieran (kee-see-EHR-ahn)

Using *querer* in the imperfect subjunctive is a polite way of asking for something. For example:

Quisiera un vaso de agua, por favor.
I would like a glass of water, please.

Quisiéramos ver la carta, por favor.
We would like to see the menu, please.

NECESITAR: to need

yo necesito (neh-seh-SEE-toh)
tú necesitas (neh-seh-SEE-tahs)
él, ella, usted necesita (neh-seh-SEE-tah)
nosotros necesitamos (neh-seh-see-TAH-mohs)
vosotros necesitáis (neh-seh-see-TAHYS)
ellos, ellas, ustedes necesitan (neh-seh-SEE-tahn)

When you need something, don't be afraid to say it with *necesitar:*

Necesito más pan, por favor.
I need more bread, please.

Ella necesita ir al doctor.
She needs to go to the doctor.

Los niños necesitan comer menos dulces.
The children need to eat fewer sweets.

Liking and Being Liked

The verb *gustar* is a little different from other verbs. In English, you say "I like something." In Spanish, however, the expression is *me gusta*—literally, "to me, it's liked." The difference is that the subject in the Spanish sentence isn't "I"—it's what you like!

If the "liked" object is singular, use *gusta* (third person singular form). If the object is plural, use *gustan* (third person plural form).

GUSTAR: equivalent of "to like"

me gusta(n) (meh GOO-stah/stahn)
te gusta(n) (teh GOO-stah/stahn)
le gusta(n) (leh GOO-stah/stahn)
nos gusta(n) (nohs GOO-stah/stahn)
os gusta(n) (ohs GOO-stah/stahn)
les gusta(n) (lehs GOO-stah/stahn)

El café te gusta.
You like coffee. (Literally, "Coffee is pleasing to you.")

A mí no me gustan los gatos.
I don't like cats.

No nos gusta el pan.
We don't like bread.

Eating at a Restaurant

Now that we've got the verbs squared away, let's move on to reading the menu and ordering a meal.

Do I need a reservation?
¿Necesito una reservación?
neh-seh-SEE-toh OO-nah rehs-ehr-vah-see-OHN

May I see a menu?
¿Puedo ver la carta?
PWEH-do vehr lah KAHR-tah

How is this prepared?
¿Cómo se prepara esto?
KOH-moh seh preh-PAH-rah EH-stoh

What do you recommend?
¿Qúe recomienda usted?
keh reh-koh-mee-EHN-dah OO-stehd

What is this?
¿Qúe es esto?
keh ehs EH-stoh

What are today's specials?
¿Cuáles son los platos del día de hoy?
KWAH-lehs sohn lohs PLAH-tohs dehl DHEE-ah deh ohy

I'd like to try a regional dish.
Quisiera probar un plato típico de la región.
kee-see-EH-rah PROH-bahr oon PLAH-toh TEE-pee-koh
deh lah reh-hee-OHN

Can you please bring the check?
¿Me puede traer la cuenta, por favor?
meh PWEH-deh trah-EHR lah KWEHN-tah pohr fah-VOHR

Can I pay with a credit card?
¿Puedo pagar con tarjeta de crédito?
PWEH-doh pah-GAHR kohn tahr-HEH-tah deh KREH-
dee-toh

I'm a vegetarian.
Soy vegetariano/a.
sohy beh-heh-tah-ree-AH-noh/nah

I'm on a diet.
Estoy a régimen.
eh-STOHY ah REH-hee-mehn

I can't have (eat/drink) . . .
No puedo comer/tomar . . .
noh PWEH-doh COH-mehr/toh-MAHR

I'm allergic to . . .
Soy alérgico/a a . . .
soy ah-LEHR-hee-koh/kah ah

Restaurant Vocabulary

waiter/waitress	*el/la camarero/a*
	ehl/lah kah-mah-REH-roh/rah
check	*la cuenta*
	lah KWEHN-tah
table	*la mesa*
	lah MEH-sah
tablecloth	*el mantel*
	ehl mahn-TEHL
place setting	*los cubiertos*
	lohs koo-bee-EHR-tohs
fork	*el tenedor*
	ehl teh-neh-DOHR
knife	*el cuchillo*
	ehl koo-CHEE-oh
spoon	*la cuchara*
	lah coo-CHAH-rah
soup spoon	*la cuchara sopera*
	lah coo-CHAH-rah soh-PEH-rah
teaspoon	*la cucharita*
	lah coo-chah-REE-tah
cup	*la taza*
	lah TAH-sah
glass	*el vaso*
	ehl VAH-soh
wine glass	*la copa de vino*
	lah KOH-pah deh VEE-noh
plate	*el plato*
	ehl PLAH-toh

Restaurant Vocabulary (continued)

bowl	*el tazón*
	ehl tah-SOHN
napkin	*la servilleta*
	lah sehr-bee-YEH-tah
restroom	*los baños*
	lohs BAHN-yohs
tip	*la propina*
	lah proh-PEE-nah
chef	*el/la cocinero/a*
	ehl/lah koh-see-NEH-roh/rah
manager	*el/la gerente*
	ehl/lah heh-REHN-teh
entrée	*el plato principal*
	ehl PLAH-toh preen-see-PAHL
dessert	*el postre*
	ehl POHS-treh
snack	*la merienda*
	lah meh-ree-YEHN-dah
appetizer	*el aperitivo*
	ehl ah-peh-ree-TEE-voh
breakfast	*el desayuno*
	ehl deh-sahy-YOO-noh
lunch	*el almuerzo*
	ehl ahl-MWEHR-soh
dinner	*la cena*
	lah SEH-nah

What's for Dinner?

You may find the following words useful as you're trying to order food from a menu, or as you shop for ingredients at a local supermarket, grocery store, or outdoor market. To make the tables more manageable, they are organized by food type.

Adjectives to Describe Your Meal

fresh	*fresca*
	FREHS-kah
sweet	*dulce*
	DOOL-seh
sour	*agrio*
	AH-gree-oh
bland	*soso*
	SOH-soh
spicy	*picante*
	pee-KAHN-teh
hot	*caliente*
	kah-lee-YEHN-teh
cold	*frío*
	FREE-oh

Methods of Preparation

baked	*al horno*
	ahl-OHR-noh
grilled	*a la parrilla*
	ah lah pah-REE-yah
roasted	*asado*
	ah-SAH-doh

Methods of Preparation (continued)

fried	*frito*
	FREE-toh
sautéed	*salteado*
	sahl-teh-AH-doh
toasted	*tostado*
	toh-STAH-doh
raw	*crudo*
	KROO-doh
rare	*poco cocido*
	POH-koh coh-SEE-doh
medium	*a término medio*
	ah TEHR-mee-noh MEH-dee-oh
well-done	*bien cocido*
	bee-EHN coh-SEE-doh
steamed	*al vapor*
	ahl vah-POHR
chopped	*picado*
	pee-KAH-doh
burned	*quemado*
	keh-MAH-doh

General Food Groups

fish	*el pescado*
	ehl pehs-KAH-doh
shellfish	*el marisco*
	ehl mah-REES-koh
chocolate	*el chocolate*
	ehl choh-koh-LAH-teh
fat	*la grasa*
	lah GRAH-sah

dairy	*los productos lácteos*
	lohs pro-DUHK-tohs LAHK-teh-ohs
vegetable	*la verdura*
	lah vehr-DOO-rah
fruit	*la fruta*
	lah FROO-tah
grains	*los cereales*
	lohs seh-reh-AH-lehs
bread	*el pan*
	ehl pahn
meat	*la carne*
	lah KAHR-neh
poultry	*las aves de corral*
	lahs AH-vehs deh koh-RRAHL
soup	*la sopa*
	lah SOH-pah
salad	*la ensalada*
	lah ehn-sah-LAH-dah
sandwich	*el bocadillo*
(on a roll)	ehl boh-kah-DEE-yoh
sandwich	*el sándwich*
(on sliced bread)	ehl SAHND-weech

Fruit

apple	*la manzana*
	lah mahn-SAH-nah
apricot	*el albaricoque*
	ehl ahl-bah-ree-KOH-keh
banana	*la banana*
	lah bah-NAH-nah

Fruit (continued)

blueberry	*el mirtilo*
	ehl meer-TEE-loh
cantaloupe	*el melón*
	ehl meh-LOHN
cherry	*la cereza*
	lah seh-REH-sah
coconut	*el coco*
	ehl KOH-koh
date	*el dátil*
	ehl DAH-teehl
fig	*el higo*
	ehl EE-goh
grape	*la uva*
	lah OO-vah
grapefruit	*el pomelo*
	ehl poh-MEH-loh
guava	*la guayaba*
	lah gwah-YAH-bah
lemon	*el limón*
	ehl lee-MOHN
lime	*la lima*
	lah LEE-mah
mango	*el mango*
	ehl MAHN-goh
melon	*el melón*
	ehl meh-LOHN
nectarine	*la nectarina*
	lah nehk-tah-REE-nah
orange	*la naranja*
	lah nah-RAHN-hah

peach	*el durazno/el melocotón*
	ehl doo-RAHS-noh/ehl meh-loh-koh-TOHN
pear	*la pera*
	lah PEH-rah
pineapple	*el ananá/la piña*
	ehl ah-nah-NAH/lah PEEN-yah
plantain	*el plátano*
	ehl PLAH-tah-noh
plum	*la ciruela*
	lah see-roo-EH-lah
prune	*la ciruela pasa*
	lah see-roo-EH-lah PAH-sah
raisin	*la pasa de uva*
	lah PAH-sah deh OOH-vah
raspberry	*la frambuesa*
	lah frahm-BWEH-sah
strawberry	*la fresa*
	lah FREH-sah
watermelon	*la sandía*
	lah sahn-DEE-ah

Vegetables

asparagus	*los espárragos*
	lohs ehs-PAH-rrah-gohs
artichoke	*la alcachofa*
	lah ahl-kah-CHOH-fah
avocado	*el aguacate*
	ehl ah-gwah-KAH-teh
beans	*los frijoles*
	lohs free-HOH-lehs

Vegetables (continued)

beet	*la remolacha*	
	lah reh-moh-LAH-chah	
broccoli	*el brécol*	
	ehl BREH-kohl	
cabbage	*la col*	
	lah kohl	
carrot	*la zanahoria*	
	lah sah-nah-OH-ree-ah	
cauliflower	*la coliflor*	
	lah koh-lee-FLOHR	
celery	*el apio*	
	ehl AH-pee-oh	
chickpeas	*los garbanzos*	
	lohs gahr-BAHN-sohs	
corn	*el maíz*	
	ehl mah-EES	
cucumber	*el pepino*	
	ehl peh-PEE-noh	
eggplant	*la berenjena*	
	lah beh-rehn-HEH-nah	
green beans	*las judías*	
	lahs hoo-DEE-ahs	
kale	*la rizada*	
	lah ree-SAH-dah	
lentils	*las lentejas*	
	lahs lehn-TEH-hahs	
lettuce	*la lechuga*	
	lah leh-CHOO-gah	
mushroom	*el champiñon*	
	ehl chahm-peen-YOHN	

onion	*la cebolla*
	lah seh-BOH-yah
peas	*los guisantes*
	lohs gee-SAHN-tehs
pepper	*el pimiento*
	ehl pee-mee-EHN-toh
potato	*la papa*
	lah PAH-pah
spinach	*la espinaca*
	lah eh-spee-NAH-kah
squash	*la calabaza*
	lah kah-lah-BAH-sah
sweet potato	*la batata/el boniato*
	lah bah-TAH-tah/ehl boh-nee-AH-toh
tomato	*el tomate*
	ehl toh-MAH-teh
zucchini	*el calabacín*
	ehl kah-lah-bah-SEEN

 FACT

Lunch, *el almuerzo*, is usually the biggest meal of the day in Spain and consists of multiple courses. In fact, it's often referred to simply as *la comida*, the meal. Dinner is generally a smaller meal and is eaten as late as ten at night.

Dairy

butter	*la mantequilla*
	lah mahn-teh-KEE-yah
cheese	*el queso*
	ehl KEH-soh
cream	*la nata*
	lah NAH-tah
egg	*el huevo*
	ehl WEH-voh
ice cream	*el helado*
	ehl eh-LAH-doh
milk	*la leche*
	lah LEH-cheh
yogurt	*el yogur*
	ehl yoh-GOOR

 ALERT!

When shopping for packaged foods in a Spanish-speaking country, remember that food weights will be labeled following the metric system.

Grains

bran	*el salvado*
	ehl sahl-VAH-doh
breakfast cereal	*el cereal del desayuno*
	ehl seh-ree-AHL dehl deh-sahy-OO-noh

flour	*la harina*
	lah ah-REE-nah
oatmeal	*los copos de avena*
	lohs KOH-pohs deh ah-VEH-nah
oats	*la avena*
	lah ah-VEH-nah
rice	*el arroz*
	ehl ah-RROHS
wheat	*el trigo*
	ehl TREE-goh

Bread

dinner roll	*el bollo*
	ehl BOH-yoh
loaf of bread	*la barra de pan*
	lah BAH-rrah deh pahn
slice of bread	*la rebanada de pan*
	lah reh-bah-NAH-dah deh pahn
toast	*el pan tostado*
	ehl pahn toh-STAH-doh
whole wheat bread	*el pan integral*
	ehl pahn een-teh-GRAHL

Meat and Poultry

beef	*la carne de vaca o de res*
	lah KAHR-neh deh BAH-kah oh deh rehs
cutlet	*la chuleta*
	lah choo-LEH-tah

Meat and Poultry (continued)

filet mignon	*el lomo fino*
	ehl LOH-moh FEE-noh
goat	*el chivo*
	ehl CHEE-voh
ham	*el jamón*
	ehl hah-MOHN
hamburger	*la hamburguesa*
	lah ahm-boor-GEH-sah
hot dog	*la salchicha*
	lah sahl-CHEE-chah
lamb	*la carne de cordero*
	lah KAHR-neh deh kohr-DEH-roh
liver	*el hígado*
	ehl HEE-gah-doh
pork	*la carne de cerdo*
	lah KAHR-neh deh SEHR-doh
roast beef	*el rosbíf*
	ehl rohs-BEEHF
sausage	*el chorizo*
	ehl choh-REE-soh
steak	*el bistec*
	ehl bee-STEHK
veal	*la carne de ternera*
	lah KAHR-neh deh tehr-NEHR-ah
chicken	*el pollo*
	ehl POH-yoh
duck	*el pato*
	ehl PAH-toh
turkey	*el pavo*
	ehl PAH-voh

ESSENTIAL

> The concept of vegetarianism isn't always widely understood in Spanish-speaking cultures. If you request a vegetarian meal, it may be assumed that you eat fish. Be sure to be specific about what you can and can't eat.

Fish and Shellfish

anchovy	*la anchoa*
	lah ahn-CHOH-ah
bass	*la merluza*
	lah mehr-LOO-sah
clam	*la almeja*
	lah ahl-MEH-hah
cod	*el bacalao*
	ehl bah-kah-LAOH
crab	*el cangrejo*
	ehl kahn-GREH-hoh
eel	*la anguila*
	lah ahn-GEE-lah
lobster	*la langosta*
	lah lahn-GOHS-tah
mussel	*el mejillón*
	ehl meh-hee-YOHN
oyster	*la ostra*
	lah OHS-trah
salmon	*el salmón*
	ehl sahl-MOHN

Fish and Shellfish (continued)

scallops	*las conchas de peregrino*
	lahs KOHN-chahs deh peh-reh-GREE-noh
shark	*el tiburón*
	ehl tee-boo-ROHN
shrimp	*las gambas*
	lahs GAHM-bahs
sole	*el lenguado*
	ehl lehn-GWAH-doh
swordfish	*el pez espada*
	ehl pehs eh-SPAH-dah
trout	*la trucha*
	lah TROO-chah
tuna	*el atún*
	ehl ah-TOON

Dessert

cake	*la torta*
	lah TOHR-tah
cookie	*la galleta*
	lah gah-YEH-tah
ice cream	*el helado*
	ehl eh-LAH-doh
pie	*el pastel*
	ehl pah-STEHL
pudding	*el pudín*
	ehl poo-DEEN
rice pudding	*el arroz con leche*
	ehl ah-RROHS kohn LEH-cheh

Beverages

alcohol	*el alcohol*
	ehl AHL-kohl
beer	*la cerveza*
	lah sehr-BEH-sah
champagne	*el champán*
	ehl chahm-PAHN
coffee	*el café*
	ehl kah-FEH
hot chocolate	*el chocolate*
	ehl choh-koh-LAH-teh
juice	*el jugo*
	ehl HOO-goh
milk	*la leche*
	lah LEH-cheh
milk shake	*el batido*
	ehl bah-TEE-doh
mineral water	*el agua mineral*
	ehl AH-gwah mee-neh-RAHL
rum	*el ron*
	ehl rohn
sherry	*el jerez*
	ehl heh-REHS
soda	*la gaseosa*
	lah gah-seh-OH-sah
tea	*el té*
	ehl teh
water	*el agua*
	ehl AH-gwah

Beverages (continued)

carbonated water	*el agua con gas*
	ehl AH-gwah kohn gahs
noncarbonated water	*el agua sin gas*
	ehl AH-gwah seen gahs
wine	*el vino*
	ehl VEE-noh

Food Shopping

If you've decided to skip the restaurant and head out to the local shops to buy groceries, you'll need to figure out where the shops are. And to do that, you have to know what they're called in Spanish.

Types of Food Stores

grocery store	*el colmado*
	ehl kohl-MAH-doh
butcher shop	*la carnicería*
	lah kahr-nee-seh-REE-ah
bakery	*la panadería*
	lah pah-nah-deh-REE-ah
delicatessen	*la salchichonería*
	lah sahl-chee-choh-neh-REE-ah
supermarket	*el supermercado*
	ehl soo-pehr-mehr-KAH-doh
pastry shop	*la pastelería*
	lah pah-steh-leh-REE-ah
fish shop	*la pescadería*
	lah peh-skah-deh-REE-ah
ice cream shop	*la heladería*
	lah eh-lah-deh-REE-ah

Once in the store, it'll help if you can ask for specific ingredients.

How Much Do You Want?

a little bit	*un poco*
	oon POH-koh
a lot	*mucho*
	MOO-choh
a bite of	*un pincho de*
	oon PEEN-choh deh
an order of	*una ración de*
	OO-nah rah-see-OHN deh
a box of	*una caja de*
	OO-nah KAH-hah deh
a bag of	*una bolsa de*
	OO-nah BOHL-sah deh
a can of	*una lata de*
	OO-nah LAH-tah deh
a jar of	*un tarro de*
	oon TAH-rroh deh
a bottle of	*una botella de*
	OO-nah boh-TEH-yah deh
a sack of	*un saco de*
	oon SAH-koh deh

Now that you've eaten your fill, let's head back out there and go shopping! In the next chapter we've got you covered with all the sizes, colors, and vocabulary you'll need for your consumer adventures in Spanish.

Chapter 8
Shop Till You Drop

Is shopping a favorite recreational activity for you? Do you want to find some souvenirs to remember your travels by? Or perhaps the airline lost your suitcase and you're just desperate to get out of that same outfit you've been wearing three days straight! Whatever your reason, going shopping will be much easier if you know how to ask for what you want.

Spring into Action

First, you'll want a few more verbs. As you learn these verbs, don't just file them into the "verbs for shopping" compartment in your brain and leave them there. Each vocabulary word you pick up in this book is a building block. As you gain confidence in Spanish, you'll be able to reuse and rearrange your words to say whatever you need to say.

- *buscar:* to look for
- *comprar:* to buy
- *llevar:* to carry, to wear
- *vender:* to sell

BUSCAR: to look for

yo busco (BOO-skoh)
tú buscas (BOO-skahs)
él, ella, usted busca (BOO-skah)
nosotros buscamos (boo-SKAH-mohs)
vosotros buscáis (boo-SKAHYS)
ellos, ellas, ustedes buscan (BOO-skahn)

¿Qué busca usted?
What are you looking for?

Busco una camiseta roja.
I'm looking for a red t-shirt.

Buscamos a Cindy.
We're looking for Cindy.

COMPRAR: to buy

yo compro (KOHM-proh)
tú compras (KOHM-prahs)
él, ella, usted compra (KOHM-prah)
nosotros compramos (kohm-PRAH-mohs)
vosotros compráis (kohm-PRAHYS)
ellos, ellas, ustedes compran (KOHM-prahn)

Él compra pan y huevos en el supermercado.
He buys bread and eggs at the supermarket.

Marla y yo compramos zapatos.
Marla and I buy shoes.

¿Qué marca de vaqueros compras?
What brand of jeans do you buy?

 FACT

> When shopping for clothes outside of the
> United States, you'll need to know the foreign
> equivalents to U.S. clothing sizes. Conversion
> charts are easy to find online. You might want
> to print one out and bring it with you if you
> think you'll be shopping for clothes during
> your trip.

LLEVAR: to carry, to wear
yo llevo (YEH-voh)
tú llevas (YEH-vahs)
él, ella, usted lleva (YEH-vah)
nosotros llevamos (yeh-VAH-mohs)
vosotros lleváis (yeh-VAHYS)
ellos, ellas, ustedes llevan (YEH-vahn)

¿Qué llevas en tu bolsa?
What do you carry in your purse?

Llevo un paraguas cuando llueve.
I carry an umbrella when it rains.

Los niños no llevan pantalones cortos en la escuela.
The children don't wear shorts in school.

VENDER: to sell
yo vendo (VEHN-doh)
tú vendes (VEHN-dahs)
él, ella, usted vende (VEHN-deh)
nosotros vendemos (vehn-DEH-mohs)
vosotros vendéis (vehn-DEHYS)
ellos, ellas, ustedes venden (VEHN-dehn)

¿Vende usted revistas en inglés?
Do you sell magazines in English?

Venden vestidos bonitos en esta tienda.
They sell pretty dresses in this store.

¿Dónde se venden antigüedades?
Where do they sell antiques?

From Shop to Shop

You never know which shop you might need to visit. For instance, the tobacco shop may come in handy even if you don't smoke. Often, it's the best place to find stamps and weekly or monthly bus and metro passes.

Types of Shops

antique shop	*el anticuario*
	ehl ahn-tee-KWAH-ree-oh
bookstore	*la librería*
	lah lee-breh-REE-ah
camera shop	*la tienda de fotografía*
	lah tee-EHN-dah deh foh-toh-grah-FEE-ah
clothing store	*la tienda de ropa*
	lah tee-EHN-dah deh ROH-pah
department store	*el almacén*
	ehl ahl-mah-SEHN
jewelry store	*la joyería*
	lah hoy-eh-REE-ah
pharmacy	*la farmacia*
	lah fahr-MAH-see-ah
record store	*la tienda de discos*
	lah tee-EHN-dah deh DEES-kohs
shoe store	*la zapatería*
	lah sah-pah-teh-REE-ah

Types of Shops (continued)

stationery store	*la papelería* lah pah-peh-leh-REE-ah
tobacco shop	*el estanquillo* ehl eh-stahn-KEE-yoh

Getting What You Need

Once you find the shop you need, you'll need to communicate with the shopkeeper. Here are a few general questions and phrases:

Can you help me?
¿Puede usted ayudarme?
PWEH-deh OO-stehd ah-yoo-DAHR-me

I'm looking for . . .
Busco . . .
BOO-skoh

Where can I find . . . ?
¿Dónde puedo encontrar . . . ?
DOHN-deh PWEH-doh ehn-kohn-TRAHR

Are there any sales?
¿Hay rebajas?
ahy reh-BAH-hahs

Do you sell . . .
¿Vende usted . . . ?
VEHN-deh OO-stehd

Could you please deliver it to my hotel?
¿Puede enviarlo a mi hotel?
PWEH-deh ehn-vee-AHR-loh ah mee OH-tehl

Can I return it?
¿Puedo devolverlo?
PWEH-doh deh-vohl-VEHR-loh

 ESSENTIAL

> It's impossible to overstate this point:
> Courtesy is valued in Spanish-speaking coun-
> tries, and you'll get much better service if you
> treat people with respect. Remember to say
> *por favor* and *gracias!*

Do you have a smaller/larger size?
¿Tiene un tamaño más pequeño/grande?
tee-EHN-eh oon tah-MAH-nyoh mahs peh-KEH-nyoh/
GRAHN-deh

I wear a size . . .
Uso un talle . . .
OO-soh oon TAH-yeh

Do you have it in other colors?
¿Lo tiene en otros colores?
loh tee-EHN-eh ehn OH-trohs koh-LOH-rehs

I'd like to try it on.
Me gustaría probármelo.
meh goos-tah-REE-ah proh-BAHR-meh-loh

I like it. / I don't like it.
Me gusta. / No me gusta.
meh GOO-stah / noh meh GOO-stah

 ALERT!

> There's no need to add the word "for" (*por*)
> after the verb *buscar* when you want to say
> "to look for." It's implied in the use of the
> verb. If you want to say I'm looking for a shirt,
> all you need to say is, *Yo busco una camisa.*

I'll buy it.
Lo compro.
loh KOHM-proh

It fits me well.
Me queda bien.
eh KEH-dah bee-EHN

It fits you well.
Te queda bien.
teh KEH-dah bee-EHN

It doesn't fit me.
No me queda bien.
noh meh KEH-dah bee-EHN

Can I pay with credit card?
¿Puedo pagar con tarjeta de crédito?
PWEH-doh pah-GAHR kohn tahr-HEH-tah deh KREH-dee-toh

How much does it cost?
¿Cúanto cuesta?
KWAHN-toh KWEH-stah

It's too expensive.
Es demasiado caro.
ehs deh-mah-see-AH-doh KAH-roh

Colors

color	*color*
	koh-LOHR
beige	*beige*
	behj
black	*negro*
	NEH-groh
blue	*azul*
	ah-SOOL
brown	*marrón, café*
	mah-RROHN, kah-FEH
gold	*dorado*
	doh-RAH-doh

Colors (continued)

gray	gris	grees
green	*verde*	VEHR-deh
orange	*naranja*	nah-RAHN-hah
pink	*rosa*	ROH-sah
purple	*morado*	moh-RAH-doh
red	rojo	ROH-hoh
silver	*plateado*	plah-teh-AH-doh
white	*blanco*	BLAHN-koh
yellow	*amarillo*	ah-mah-REE-yoh
light	*claro*	KLAH-roh
dark	*oscuro*	oh-SKOO-roh
striped	*rayado*	rah-YAH-doh
plaid	*escocés*	ehs-koh-SEHS

Expressing Your Opinion

pretty	*bonito/a*
	boh-NEE-toh/ah
ugly	*feo/a*
	FEH-oh/ah
short	*bajo/a*
	BAH-hoh/ah
long	*largo/a*
	LAHR-goh/ah
inexpensive	*barato/a*
	bah-RAH-toh/ah
expensive	*caro/a*
	KAH-roh/ah
loose	*ancho/a*
	AHN-choh/ah
tight	*estrecho/a*
	eh-STREH-choh/ah
thin	*delgado/a, fino/a*
	dehl-GAH-doh/ah, FEE-noh/ah
thick	*grueso/a*
	groo-EH-soh/ah
small	*pequeño/a*
	peh-KEH-nyoh/ah
medium	*mediano/a*
	meh-dee-AH-noh/ah
large	*grande*
	GRAHN-deh
smaller	*más pequeño/a*
	mahs peh-KEH-nyoh/ah

Expressing Your Opinion (continued)

larger	*más grande*
	mahs GRAHN-deh
shorter	*más corto/a*
	mahs KOHR-toh/ah
longer	*más largo/a*
	mahs LAHR-goh/ah
less expensive	*más barato/a*
	mahs bah-RAH-toh/ah
better	*mejor*
	meh-HOHR
worse	*peor*
	peh-OHR
too small	*demasiado pequeño/a*
	deh-mah-see-AH-doh peh-KEH-nyoh/ah
too big	*demasiado grande*
	deh-mah-see-AH-doh GRAHN-deh

Clothing and Jewelry

Let's start with the basics—shopping for clothes, *ropa* (ROH-pah).

Clothing

bathing suit	*el traje de baño*
	ehl TRAH-heh deh BAH-nyoh
belt	*el cinturón*
	ehl seen-too-ROHN
blouse	*la blusa*
	lah BLOO-sah

boots	*las botas*
	lahs BOH-tahs
bra	*el sostén*
	ehl sohs-TEHN
cap	*el gorro*
	ehl GOH-rroh
coat	*el abrigo*
	ehl ah-BREE-goh
dress	*el vestido*
	ehl veh-STEE-doh
gloves	*los guantes*
	lohs GWAHN-tehs
hat	*el sombrero*
	ehl sohm-BREH-roh
jacket	*la chaqueta*
	lah chah-KEH-tah
jeans	*los vaqueros*
	lohs bah-KEH-rohs
panties	*las bragas*
	lahs BRAH-gahs
pants	*los pantalones*
	lohs pahn-tah-LOH-nehs
pantyhose	*las pantimedias*
	lahs pahn-tee-MEH-dee-ahs
sandals	*las sandalias*
	lahs sahn-DAH-lee-ahs
scarf	*la bufanda*
	lah boo-FAHN-dah
shirt	*la camisa*
	lah kah-MEE-sah

Clothing and Jewelry (continued)

shoes	*los zapatos*
	lohs sah-PAH-tohs
shorts	*los pantalones cortos*
	lohs pahn-tah-LOH-nehs KOHR-tohs
skirt	*la falda*
	lah FAHL-dah
socks	*los calcetines*
	lohs kahl-seh-TEE-nehs
stockings	*las medias*
	lahs MEH-dee-ahs
suit	*el traje*
	ehl TRAH-heh
t-shirt	*la camiseta*
	lah kah-mee-SEH-tah
tie	*la corbata*
	lah kohr-BAH-tah
underpants	*los calzoncillos*
	lohs kahl-sohn-SEE-ohs
underwear	*la ropa interior*
	lah ROH-pah een-teh-ree-OHR
vest	*el chaleco*
	ehl chah-LEH-koh

Fabrics

alpaca	*la alpaca*
	lah ahl-PAH-kah
angora	*la angora*
	lah ahn-GOH-rah

cashmere	*la cachemira*
	lah kah-cheh-MEE-rah
corduroy	*la pana*
	lah PAH-nah
cotton	*el algodón*
	ehl ahl-goh-DOHN
crepe	*el crespón*
	ehl krehs-POHN
denim	*el dril*
	ehl dreel
lace	*el encaje*
	ehl ehn-KAH-heh
leather	*el cuero*
	ehl KWEH-roh
linen	*el lino*
	ehl LEE-noh
muslin	*la muselina*
	lah moo-seh-LEE-nah
nylon	*el nilon*
	ehl NEE-lohn
polyester	*el poliéster*
	ehl poh-lee-EHS-tehr
rayon	*el rayón*
	ehl rah-YOHN
silk	*la seda*
	lah SEH-dah
suede	*el ante*
	ehl AHN-teh
velvet	*el terciopelo*
	ehl TEHR-see-oh-PEH-loh

Fabrics (continued)

wool   *la lana*
           lah LAH-nah

Now that you've got a full outfit, how about some jewelry to match?

Jewelry

bracelet	*la pulsera*
	lah pool-SEH-rah
earrings	*los pendientes*
	lohs pehn-dee-EHN-tehs
necklace	*el collar*
	ehl koh-YAHR
ring	*el anillo*
	ehl ah-NEE-yoh
gold	*el oro*
	ehl OH-roh
silver	*la plata*
	lah PLAH-tah
platinum	*el platino*
	ehl plah-TEE-noh
diamond	*el diamante*
	ehl dee-ah-MAHN-teh
emerald	*la esmeralda*
	lah ehs-meh-RAHL-dah
sapphire	*el zafiro*
	eh sah-FEE-roh
ruby	*el rubí*
	ehl roo-BEE

topaz	*el topacio*
	ehl toh-PAH-see-yoh
turquoise	*la turquesa*
	lah toor-KEH-sah

Something to Read

Even if you don't know enough Spanish to be able to read a book or make sense of a magazine article, don't worry. Some bookshops and magazine kiosks carry English-language publications—all you need to do is ask:

Do you have books/magazines/newspapers in English?
¿Tiene libros/revistas/periódicos en inglés?
tee-EHN-eh   LEE-brohs/reh-VEE-stahs/peh-ree-OH-dee-kohs ehn een-GLEHS

Do you sell guide books?
¿Vende usted guías turísticas?
VEHN-deh OO-stehd GEE-ahs too-REE-stee-kahs

Books and Stationery

book	*el libro*
	ehl LEE-broh
newspaper	*el periódico*
	ehl peh-ree-OH-dee-koh
magazine	*la revista*
	lah reh-VEE-stah
paper	*el papel*
	ehl pah-PEHL

Books and Stationery (continued)

notebook	*el cuaderno* ehl kwah-DEHR-noh
envelope	*el sobre* ehl SOH-breh
postcard	*la tarjeta postal* lah tahr-HEH-tah POH-stahl
fiction	*la ficción* lah feek-see-OHN
nonfiction	*la literatura no novelesca* lah lee-teh-rah-TOO-rah noh noh-veh-LEH-skah
novel	*la novela* lah noh-VEH-lah
biography	*la biografía* lah bee-oh-grah-FEE-ah
children's books	*los libros para niños* lohs LEE-brohs PAH-rah NEE-nyohs
poetry	*la poesía* lah poh-eh-SEE-ah
pen	*la pluma* lah PLOO-mah
pencil	*el lápiz* ehl LAH-pees

Music to My Ears

Why not explore the wide variety of sounds in Latin music? Try some *cante jondo* and classical guitar from Spain, some *salsa* and *merengue* from South America and the Caribbean, or maybe *tejano* from the American

Southwest. You don't have to travel too far from home to experience the sounds of the varied Latin cultures. In fact, you can even find traditional Andean musical groups in the subway stations of New York City and buy a CD from them while you're at it!

I'd like to buy some traditional music of the region.
Quisiera comprar música tradicional de la región.
kee-see-EH-rah kohm-PRAHR MOO-see-kah trah-dee-see-oh-NAHL deh lah reh-hee-OHN

Do you have albums by local musicians?
¿Tiene álbumes de músicos locales?
tee-EHN-eh AHL-boo-mehs deh MOO-see-kohs loh-KAH-les

Can I listen to this before I buy it?
¿Puedo escucharlo antes de comprar?
PWEH-doh eh-skoo-CHAR-loh AHN-tehs deh kohm-PRAHR

Music

music	*la música*
	lah MOO-see-kah
album	*el álbum*
	ehl AHL-boom
cassette tape	*la cinta*
	lah SEEN-tah
compact disc	*el disco compacto*
	ehl DEE-skoh kohm-PAHK-toh
musician	*el músico*
	ehl MOO-see-koh

Music (continued)

singer	*el/la cantante*
	ehl/lah kahn-TAHN-teh
guitarist	*el/la guitarrista*
	ehl/lah gee-tah-RREE-stah
pianist	*el/la pianista*
	ehl/lah pee-ah-NEE-stah

It's hard work, all that shopping! Now it's time for play. The next chapter is all about entertainment, from taking in a movie to a night of dancing.

 QUESTION?

If a bookstore is *una librería*, then what's the Spanish word for "library"?
The Spanish word for library is *biblioteca*. *Librería* is a false cognate.

Chapter 9

Out on the Town

Y ou're getting pretty good at this Spanish phrase thing and you want to hit the town to celebrate. In this chapter, you'll learn some vocabulary that will add to the fun as you go out to the movies, theater, dancing, or the local bar.

Verbs at Play

Remember, verbs are words of action! Here are some playtime verbs to take with you for a night out on the town.

BAILAR: to dance

yo bailo (BAHY-loh)
tú bailas (BAHY-lahs)
él, ella, usted baila (BAHY-lah)
nosotros bailamos (bahy-LAH-mohs)
vosotros bailáis (bahy-LAHYS)
ellos, ellas, ustedes bailan (BAHY-lahn)

¡Qué bien baila usted!
You dance so well!

Bailamos juntos.
We dance together.

CANTAR: to sing

yo canto (KAHN-toh)
tú cantas (KAHN-tahs)
él, ella, usted canta (KAHN-tah)
nosotros cantamos (kahn-TAH-mohs)
vosotros cantáis (kahn-TAHYS)
ellos, ellas, ustedes cantan (KAHN-tahn)

Marlena canta en el coro.
Marlena sings in the choir.

Canto villancicos en Navidad.
I sing carols at Christmastime.

MIRAR: to watch

yo miro (MEE-roh)
tú miras (MEE-rahs)
él, ella, usted mira (MEE-rah)
nosotros miramos (mee-RAH-mohs)
vosotros miráis (mee-RAHYS)
ellos, ellas, ustedes miran (MEE-rahn)

Ustedes miran dibujos animados todo el día.
You watch cartoons all day.

¡Mira por allá!
Look over there! (informal)

 FACT

> Listening to music with Spanish lyrics is a great
> way to build your listening skills and colloquial
> vocabulary. Salsa is great, but it's not the only
> game in town. Also check out *bachata*, *cumbia*,
> and *merengue*, among many others.

At the Movies

Watching movies in a foreign language is a great way to
pick up new words and get the sound of the language
in your ear. Why not go see a movie in Spanish with
English subtitles and see how much you can understand
without resorting to reading? You may surprise yourself!

Cinema Vocabulary

cinema	*el cine*
	ehl SEE-neh
screen	*la pantalla*
	lah pahn-TAH-yah
ticket	*la entrada*
	lah ehn-TRAH-dah
movie	*la película*
	lah peh-LEE-koo-lah
popcorn	*las palomitas*
	lahs pah-loh-MEE-tahs
candy	*los caramelos*
	lohs kah-rah-MEH-lohs
seat	*el asiento*
	ehl ah-see-YEHN-toh
aisle	*el pasillo*
	ehl pah-SEE-yoh
action movie	*la película de acción*
	lah peh-LEE-koo-lah deh ahk-see-OHN
comedy	*la comedia*
	lah koh-MEH-dee-ah
romance	*la película de amor*
	lah peh-LEE-koo-lah deh ah-MOHR
mystery	*el misterio*
	ehl mee-STEH-ree-yoh
science fiction	*la película de ciencia ficción*
	lah peh-LEE-koo-lah deh see-EHN-see-yah feek-see-OHN

Do you want to go to the movies?
¿Quieres ir al cine?
kee-EH-rehs eer ahl SEE-neh

What time does the movie start?
¿Cuándo empieza la película?
KWAHN-doh ehm-pee-EH-sah lah peh-LEE-koo-lah

Are there English subtitles?
¿Hay subtítulos en inglés?
ahy soob-TEE-too-lohs ehn een-GLEHS

I'd like two tickets, please.
Quisiera dos entradas, por favor.
kee-see-EH-rah dohs ehn-TRAH-dahs pohr fah-VOHR

 ALERT!

> If you're traveling in a place where you can't
> drink the water, remember that includes the
> ice cubes in your drink! After a few cocktails,
> this point is easily forgotten, but if you do,
> you might develop something more than just
> a hangover the next day.

At the Theater

A night at the theater in a new city can be quite
exciting. No subtitles at the theater, though, so it will be
a real challenge—unless you go to the ballet!

Theater Vocabulary

theater	*el teatro*
	ehl teh-AH-troh
stage	*la escena*
	lah eh-SEH-nah
curtain	*el telón*
	ehl teh-LOHN
actor	*el actor*
	ehl ahk-TOHR
actress	*la actriz*
	lah ahk-TREES
play	*la obra de teatro*
	lah OH-brah deh teh-AH-troh
monologue	*el monólogo*
	ehl moh-NOH-loh-goh
intermission	*el entreacto*
	ehl ehn-treh-AHC-toh

Dancing at a Nightclub

Ah, music, the international language. Once it starts, you're right at home in any language, right? Good for you. Ladies, do please note that if you're in a salsa club you may encounter a custom known as *sacar a bailar*. A man may grab your hand and pull you toward the dance floor. Feel free to say "no," but don't be offended and overreact. It's all just a part of the salsa game.

Nightclub Vocabulary

music	*la música*
	lah MOO-see-kah
song	*una canción*
	OO-nah kahn-see-OHN
dance floor	*la pista de baile*
	lah PEE-stah deh BAHY-leh

Is there an admission charge?
¿Es necesario pagar la entrada?
ehs neh-seh-SAH-ree-oh pah-GAHR lah ehn-TRAH-dah

Would you like to dance?
¿Quisieras bailar?
kee-see-EH-rahs bahy-LAHR

I don't want to dance, thank you.
No quiero bailar, gracias.
noh kee-EH-roh bahy-LAHR, GRAH-see-ahs

At the Bar

Bars can provide a good opportunity to meet new people and practice your language skills. Afraid of ordering the wrong thing and ending up with a glass of mystery liquid? Never fear. Here's some bar vocabulary to help you out.

Bar Vocabulary

bar	*el bar*
	ehl bahr
bartender	*el cantinero*
	ehl kahn-tee-NEH-roh
beer	*la cerveza*
	lah sehr-VEH-sah
wine	*el vino*
	ehl VEE-noh
alcohol	*el alcohol*
	ehl ahl-KOHL
bottle of beer	*la botella de cerveza*
	lah boh-TEHY-yah deh sehr-VEH-sah
glass of beer	*el vaso de cerveza*
	ehl VAH-soh deh sehr-VEH-sah
bourbon	*el bourbon*
	ehl boor-BOHN
gin	*la ginebra*
	lah hee-NEH-brah

And here's one last phrase you might need:

Can I buy you a drink?
¿Puedo comprarte una bebida?
PWEH-doh kohm-PRAHR-teh OO-nah beh-BEE-dah

Okay, that's enough fun and games for one chapter. Now, on to Chapter 10, where we get down to *negocios*.

Chapter 10
Spanish for Business

As our world gets smaller and more diverse, the workplace follows suit. Spanish is an asset in the workplace, now more than ever. Whether you work in a doctor's office in New York or a construction site in Miami, there are probably times when a bit of *español* would make your job a bit easier.

Verbs That Work

We work for the money, right? Sure, sure, lottery winners always say they won't quit their jobs, but you KNOW they're lying. So here are the big verbs you'll need in this arena.

- *pagar:* to pay
- *planear:* to plan, schedule
- *trabajar:* to work

 FACT

> Just as Spanish has seeped into everyday American English, so has English worked its way into Spanish, particularly in regards to technological terms. You may be surprised by how many cognates there are within this area.

PAGAR: to pay

yo pago (PAH-goh)
tú pagas (PAH-gahs)
él, ella, usted paga (PAH-gah)
nosotros pagamos (pah-GAH-mohs)
vosotros pagáis (pah-GAHYS)
ellos, ellas, ustedes pagan (PAH-gahn)

El trabajo paga diez dólares por hora.
The job pays ten dollars an hour.

Págame mañana.
Pay me tomorrow.

Cuando vamos al restaurante, ellos siempre pagan.
They always pay when we go to a restaurant.

PLANEAR: to plan, to schedule

yo planeo (plah-NEH-oh)
tú planeas (plah-NEH-ahs)
él, ella, usted planea (plah-NEH-ah)
nosotros planeamos (plah-neh-AH-mohs)
vosotros planeáis (plah-neh-AHYS)
ellos, ellas, ustedes planean (plah-NEH-ahn)

Nosotros planeamos el calendario para el mes próximo.
We are planning out the schedule for the next month.

Carlos planea su viaje de negocios.
Carlos is planning his business trip.

TRABAJAR: to work

yo trabajo (trah-BAH-hoh)
tú trabajas (trah-BAH-hahs)
él, ella, usted trabaja (trah-BAH-hah)
nosotros trabajamos (trah-bah-HAH-mohs)
vosotros trabajáis (trah-bah-HAHYS)
ellos, ellas, ustedes trabajan (trah-BAH-hahn)

¿Dónde trabajáis?
Where do you all work?

Trabajo cinco días a la semana.
I work five days a week.

Ella trabaja media jornada.
She works part-time.

 ALERT!

> Different cultures have different working
> hours and expectations. Whether you're the
> employer or the employee, be sure to clarify
> the working hours up front.

Help Wanted

Whether you're in charge of hiring, or you're the one
applying for a job, the following words and phrases can
help you make sense of the process.

Looking for Work

job	*el trabajo*
	ehl trah-BAH-hoh
boss	*el/la jefe/a*
	ehl/lah HEH-feh/ah
employee	*el/la empleado/a*
	ehl/lah ehm-pleh-YAH-doh/dah

I'm looking for a job.
Busco trabajo.
BOOH-skoh trah-BAH-hoh

Here is my resume.
Aquí está mi hoja de vida/curriculum.
ah-KEE eh-STAH mee OH-hah deh VEE-dah/coo-REE-coo-loom

Here are my references.
Aquí tiene una lista de mis referencias.
ah-KEE TEE-eh-neh OO-nah LEE-stah deh mees reh-feh-REHN-see-ahs

I'm a high school graduate.
Soy titulado del colegio.
soy tee-too-LAH-doh dehl koh-LEH-hee-oh

I'm a college graduate.
Soy graduado de la universidad.
soy grah-doo-AH-doh deh lah oo-nee-vehr-see-DAHD

I'd like to work part-time.
Quisiera trabajar media jornada.
kee-see-EH-rah trah-bah-HAHR MEH-dee-ah hohr-NAH-dah

I'd like to work full-time.
Quisiera trabajar tiempo completo.
kee-see-EH-rah trah-bah-HAHR tee-EHM-poh cohm-PLEH-toh

Do you offer health insurance?
¿Ofrece seguro médico?
oh-FREH-seh seh-GOO-roh MEH-dee-koh

I have . . . years of experience.
Tengo . . . años de experiencia.
TEHN-goh . . . AH-nyohs deh ehk-speh-ree-EHN-see-ah

I have working papers.
Tengo permiso de trabajo.
TEHN-goh pehr-MEE-soh deh trah-bah-HOH

I don't have working papers.
No tengo permiso de trabajo.
noh TEHN-goh pehr-MEE-soh deh trah-bah-HOH

May I see your resume?
¿Puedo ver su hoja de vida?
PWEH-doh vehr soo OH-HAH deh VEE-dah

Are there references I can contact?
¿Tiene referencias que pueda llamar?
tee-EH-neh reh-feh-REHN-see-ahs keh PWEH-dah YAH-mahr

Do you have working papers?
¿Tiene permiso de trabajo?
tee-EH-neh ehl pehr-MEE-soh deh trah-bah-HOH

How much experience do you have?
¿Cuánta experiencia tiene?
KWAHN-tah ehk-speh-ree-EHN-see-ah tee-EH-neh

How long have you worked in this field?
¿Cuánto tiempo lleva trabajando en este especialidad?
KWAHN-toh tee-EHM-poh YEH-vah trah-bah-HAHN-doh ehn
EH-steh ehs-peh-see-ah-lee-DAHD

When can you start?
¿Cuándo puede empezar?
KWAHN-doh PWEH-deh ehm-peh-SAHR

Pay Day

money	*el dinero*
	ehl dee-NEH-roh
cash	*el efectivo*
	ehl eh-fehk-TEE-voh
check	*el cheque*
	ehl CHEH-keh
I pay . . . an hour.	*Pago . . . la hora.*
	PAH-goh . . . lah OH-rah
per day	*al día*
	ahl DEE-ah
per week	*a la semana*
	ah lah seh-MAH-nah
per month	*al mes*
	ahl MEHS
plus room and board	*más cuarto y comida*
	mahs KWAHR-toh ee koh-MEE-dah
I'll pay you on . . .	*Le pagaré el . . .*
	leh pah-gah-REH ehl

Working Schedule

Be here at . . .
Esté aquí a las . . .
eh-STEH ah-KEE ah lahs

Stop work at . . .
Para a las . . .
PAH-rah ah lahs

Start work at . . .
Empiece a trabajar a las . . .
ehm-pee-EH-seh ah trah-bah-HAHR ah lahs

You can leave at . . .
Se puede ir a las . . .
seh PWEH-deh eer ah lahs

You'll have Sundays off.
Descansará los domingos.
dehs-kahn-sah-RAH lohs doh-MEEN-gohs

You must wear a uniform.
Tiene que usar un uniforme.
tee-EHN-eh keh OO-sahr oon oo-nee-FOHR-meh

You must wear safety gear.
Tiene que usar avíos de seguridad.
tee-EHN-eh keh OO-sahr ah-VEE-yohs deh seh-goo-ree-DAHD

Do it like this.
Hágalo así.
AH-gah-loh ah-SEE

Follow me.
Sígame.
SEE-gah-meh

 ESSENTIAL

> No, you can't just show up in a foreign country
> and get a job. You'll need working papers, or
> *permiso de trabajar.* If you think you're going
> to want to work while abroad, check with that
> country's embassy before you leave the United
> States to find out what the requirements are
> to work legally.

Workplace Vocabulary

Here are vocabulary terms specific to four common
workplaces. Combine these with related chapters to sup-
plement the information here.

At the Office

calculator	*la calculadora*
	lah kahl-koo-lah-DOHR-ah
computer	*el ordenador/la computadora*
	ehl ohr-deh-nah-DOHR/lah com-
	poo-tah-DOH-rah

At the Office (continued)

desk	*el escritorio*
	ehl ehs-kree-TOHR-ee-oh
disk	*el disquete*
	ehl dees-KEH-teh
envelope	*el sobre*
	ehl SOH-breh
eraser	*la goma*
	lah GOH-mah
fax machine	*el fax*
	ehl fahks
glue	*el pegamento*
	ehl peh-gah-MEHN-toh
message	*el mensaje*
	ehl mehn-SAH-heh
paper	*el papel*
	ehl pah-PEHL
paperclip	*el sujetapapeles*
	ehl soo-HEH-tah-pah-PEHL-ehs
pen	*la pluma*
	lah PLOO-mah
pencil	*el lápiz*
	ehl LAH-pees
pencil sharpener	*el sacapuntas*
	ehl sah-kah-POON-tahs
photocopier	*la fotocopiadora*
	lah foh-toh-koh-pee-ah-DOH-rah
printer	*la impresora*
	lah eem-preh-SOH-rah
stapler	*la grapadora*
	lah grah-pah-DOHR-ah

stamp	*el sello*
	ehl SEH-yoh
tape	*la cinta adhesiva*
	lah SEEN-tah ahd-heh-SEE-vah
telephone	*el teléfono*
	ehl teh-LEH-foh-noh
to type	*escribir a máquina*
	ehs-kree-BEER ah MAH-kee-nah
writing pad	*el bloc*
	ehl blohk

At the Construction Site

blowtorch	*el soplete*
	ehl soh-PLEH-teh
boots	*las botas*
	lahs BOH-tahs
ceiling	*el techo*
	ehl TEH-choh
cement	*el cemento*
	ehl seh-MEHN-toh
drill	*el taladro*
	ehl tah-LAH-doh
dust	*el polvo*
	ehl POHL-boh
floor	*el suelo*
	ehl SWEH-loh
gloves	*los guantes*
	lohs GWAHN-tehs
hammer	*el martillo*
	ehl mahr-TEE-yoh

At the Construction Site (continued)

ladder	*la escalera de mano*
	lah ehs-kah-LEH-rah deh MAH-noh
level	*el nivel*
	ehl nee-VEHL
nail	*el clavo*
	ehl KLAH-boh
paint	*la pintura*
	lah peen-TOO-rah
paintbrush	*la brocha*
	lah BROH-chah
plywood	*la madera contrachapada*
	lah mah-DEH-rah kohn-trah-chah-PAH-dah
roof	*el tejado*
	ehl teh-HAH-doh
ruler	*la regla*
	lah REH-glah
safety goggles	*las gafas protectoras*
	lahs GAH-fahs proh-tehk-TOH-rahs
saw	*la sierra*
	lah see-YEH-rrah
screw	*el tornillo*
	ehl tohr-NEE-yoh
shovel	*la pala*
	lah PAH-lah
steel	*el acero*
	ehl ah-SEH-roh
tape measure	*la cinta métrica*
	lah SEEN-tah MEH-tree-kah

tool	*la herramienta*
	lah heh-rrah-mee-YEHN-tah
toolbox	*la caja de herramientas*
	lah KAH-hah deh heh-rrah-mee-
	YEHN-tahs
truck	*el camión*
	ehl kah-mee-YOHN
wall (freestanding)	*el muro*
	ehl MOO-roh
wall (city)	*la muralla*
	lah moo-RAHY-yah
wheelbarrow	*la carretilla*
	lah kah-rreh-TEE-yah
wood	*la madera*
	lah mah-DEH-rah

Cleaning Service

bleach	*la lejía*
	lah leh-HEE-yah
broom	*la escoba*
	lah eh-SKOH-bah
bucket	*el cubo*
	ehl KOO-boh
carpet	*la alfombra*
	lah ahl-FOHM-brah
to clean	*limpiar*
	leem-pee-AHR
detergent	*el detergente*
	ehl deh-tehr-HEHN-teh

Cleaning Service (continued)

dirt	*la suciedad*
	lah soo-see-eh-DAHD
dirty	*sucio*
	SOO-see-oh
dust	*el polvo*
	ehl POHL-boh
to dust	*quitar el polvo*
	kee-TAHR ehl POHL-boh
floor	*el suelo*
	ehl SWEH-loh
mop	*la fregona*
	lah freh-GOH-nah
sponge	*la esponja*
	lah eh-SPOHN-hah
to sweep	*barrer*
	bah-RREHR
vacuum	*la aspiradora*
	lah ah-spee-rah-DOH-rah
to vacuum	*limpiar con aspiradora*
	leem-pee-AHR kohn ah-spee-rah-DOH-rah

Food Service

bowl	*el cuenco*
	ehl KWEHN-koh
cook	*el/la cocinero/a*
	ehl/lah koh-see-NEH-roh/rah
to cook	*cocinar*
	koh-see-NAHR

dish	*el plato*
	ehl PLAH-toh
dishwasher	*el/la lavaplatos*
(person)	ehl/lah lah-vah-PLAH-tohs
dishwasher	*el lavaplatos*
(machine)	ehl lah-vah-PLAH-tohs
menu	*la carta*
	lah KAHR-tah
oven	*el horno*
	ehl OHR-noh
place setting	*el cubierto*
	ehl koo-bee-YEHR-toh
plate	*el plato*
	ehl PLAH-toh
stove	*la estufa*
	lah eh-STOO-fah
table	*la mesa*
	lah MEH-sah
waiter	*el/la camarero/a*
	ehl/lah kah-mah-REH-roh/rah

Also see Chapter 7 for a more comprehensive treatment of restaurant terms and phrases.

So you found yourself a dream job as a dive instructor in Costa Rica and promptly dropped an air tank on your toe? Check out the next chapter for the vocabulary that'll get you through that little trip to the emergency room.

QUESTION?

Will my American accent get in the way if I try to use Spanish in business situations?
No more than a non-native speaker of English would be judged for their accent if the situations were reversed. As long as you can be understood, there should be no problem.

Chapter 11

Visiting a Doctor

It's not as much fun to think about as shopping or trying some exotic new cuisine, but if you find yourself with a medical emergency (or just a common cold) while in a Spanish-speaking country, the information in this chapter will prove invaluable. And for the medical professional, this chapter will help you to treat Spanish-speaking patients who may have limited or no English-language skills.

The Body and Its Ailments

Let's start with the terms you'll need, and then work our way up to the phrases you'll use with this new vocabulary. Remember, the gender of a noun doesn't change depending on the speaker. *El estómago* remains a masculine noun, whether it's in the body of a man or woman.

General Terms

aorta	*la aorta*
	lah ah-OHR-tah
artery	*la arteria*
	lah ahr-teh-REE-ah
blood	*la sangre*
	lah SAHN-greh
body	*el cuerpo*
	ehl KWEHR-poh
bone	*el hueso*
	ehl WEH-soh
capillary	*el capilar*
	ehl kah-pee-LAHR
cartilage	*el cartílago*
	ehl kahr-TEE-lah-goh
circulation	*la circulación*
	lah seehr-koo-lah-see-OHN
hormone	*la hormona*
	lah ohr-MOH-nah
joint	*la articulación*
	lah ahr-tee-koo-lah-see-OHN
ligament	*el ligamento*
	ehl lee-gah-MEHN-toh

limb	*el miembro*
	ehl mee-EHM-broh
lymph node	*el nódulo linfático*
	ehl NOH-doo-loh leen-FAH-tee-koh
marrow	*la médula*
	lah MEH-doo-lah
mole	*el lunar*
	ehl loo-NAHR
muscle	*el músculo*
	ehl MOO-skoo-loh
nerve	*el nervio*
	ehl NEHR-bee-oh
organ	*el órgano*
	ehl OHR-gah-noh
pore	*el poro*
	ehl POH-roh
pulse	*el pulso*
	ehl POOL-soh
reflex	*el reflejo*
	ehl reh-FLEH-hoh
skeleton	*el esqueleto*
	ehl eh-SKEH-leh-toh
skin	*la piel*
	lah pee-EHL
tendon	*el tendón*
	ehl tehn-DOHN
urine	*la orina*
	lah oh-REE-nah
vein	*la vena*
	lah VEH-nah

Systems of the Body

circulatory system	*el sistema circulatorio*
	ehl sees-TEH-mah seer-koo-lah-TOH-ree-oh
digestive system	*el sistema digestivo*
	ehl sees-TEH-mah dee-heh-STEE-boh
endocrine system	*el sistema endocrino*
	ehl sees-TEH-mah ehn-doh-KREE-noh
gastrointestinal system	*el sistema gastrointestinal*
	ehl sees-TEH-mah GAH-stroh-een-tehs-tee-NAHL
nervous system	*el sistema nervioso*
	ehl sees-TEH-mah nehr-vee-OH-soh
reproductive system	*el sistema reproductivo*
	ehl sees-TEH-mah reh-proh-dook-TEE-voh
respiratory system	*el sistema respiratorio*
	ehl sees-TEH-mah reh-spee-rah-TOH-ree-oh

The Head

brain	*el cerebro*
	ehl seh-REH-broh
cheek	*la mejilla*
	lah meh-HEE-yah
chin	*el mentón*
	ehl mehn-TOHN
cranium	*el cráneo*
	ehl KRAH-neh-oh
ear	*la oreja*
	lah oh-REH-hah

eye	*el ojo*
	ehl OH-hoh
eyeball	*el globo del ojo*
	ehl GLOH-boh dehl OH-hoh
eyebrow	*la ceja*
	lah SEH-hah
eyelash	*la pestaña*
	lah peh-STAH-nyah
eyelid	*el párpado*
	ehl PAHR-pah-doh
eye socket	*la cuenca de los ojos*
	lah KWEHN-kah deh lohs OH-hohs
iris	*el iris*
	ehl EE-rees
face	*la cara*
	lah KAH-rah
forehead	*la frente*
	lah FREHN-teh
hair	*el pelo*
	ehl PEH-loh
jaw	*la mandíbula*
	lah mahn-DEE-boo-lah
lip	*el labio*
	ehl LAH-bee-yoh
mouth	*la boca*
	lah BOH-kah
neck	*el cuello*
	ehl KWEH-yoh
nose	*la nariz*
	lah nah-REES

The Head (continued)

nostril	*la fosa nasal*
	lah FOH-sah nah-SAHL
pupil	*la pupila*
	lah POO-pee-lah
retina	*la retina*
	lah REH-tee-nah
saliva	*la saliva*
	lah sah-LEE-vah
scalp	*el cuero cabelludo*
	ehl koo-EH-roh cah-beh-YEW-doh
skin	*la piel*
	lah pee-EHL
skull	*el cráneo*
	ehl KRAH-neh-yoh
tear	*la lágrima*
	lah LAH-gree-mah
temple	*la sien*
	lah SEE-yen
throat	*la garganta*
	lah gahr-GAHN-tah
tongue	*la lengua*
	lah LEHN-gwah
tonsils	*las amígdalas*
	lahs ah-MEEG-dah-lahs
tooth	*el diente*
	ehl dee-EHN-teh
trachea	*la tráquea*
	lah TRAH-keh-yah

ESSENTIAL

> Being able to tell the doctor what medical problems you have is essential—in fact, it might save your life. If you have specific allergies, heart disease, diabetes, or another health-threatening condition, make sure you memorize what it's called so you'll remember the right words in a difficult situation.

The Trunk

abdomen	*el abdomen*
	ehl AHB-doh-mehn
anus	*el ano*
	ehl AH-noh
appendix	*el apéndice*
	ehl ah-PEHN-dee-seh
back	*la espalda*
	lah eh-SPAHL-dah
belly	*la barriga*
	lah bah-RREE-gah
bladder	*la vejiga*
	lah veh-HEE-gah
breast	*el seno*
	ehl SEH-noh
buttocks	*las nalgas*
	lahs NAHL-gahs

The Trunk (continued)

cervix	*la cervix*
	lah SEHR-veeks
chest	*el pecho*
	ehl PEH-choh
collar bone	*la clavícula*
	lah klah-VEE-koo-lah
colon	*el colon*
	ehl KOH-lohn
crotch	*las entrepiernas*
	lahs ehn-treh-pee-EHR-nahs
esophagus	*el esófago*
	ehl eh-SOH-fah-goh
heart	*el corazón*
	ehl koh-rah-SOHN
hip	*la cadera*
	lah kah-DEH-rah
intestines	*los intestinos*
	lohs een-TEHS-tee-nohs
kidney	*el riñón*
	ehl reen-YOHN
liver	*el hígado*
	ehl EE-gah-doh
lung	*el pulmón*
	ehl pool-MOHN
navel	*el ombligo*
	ehl ohm-BLEE-goh
ovary	*el ovario*
	ehl oh-BAH-ree-oh
pancreas	*el páncreas*
	ehl PAHN-kreh-ahs

pelvis	*la pelvis*
	lah PEHL-vees
penis	*el pene*
	ehl PEH-neh
rectum	*el recto*
	ehl REHK-toh
rib	*la costilla*
	lah kohs-TEE-yah
shoulder	*el hombro*
	ehl OHM-broh
shoulder blade	*la espaldilla*
	lah ehs-pahl-DEE-yah
spinal column	*la columna vertebral*
	lah coh-LOOHM-nah vehr-teh-BRAHL
stomach	*el estómago*
	ehl eh-STOH-mah-goh
testicle	*el testículo*
	ehl tehs-TEE-koo-loh
urinary tract	*la vejiga de la orina*
	lah veh-HEE-gah deh la oh-REE-nah
uterus	*el útero*
	ehl OO-teh-roh
vagina	*la vagina*
	lah vah-HEE-nah
vertebra	*la vértebra*
	lah VEHR-teh-brah
waist	*la cintura*
	lah seen-TOO-rah

The Limbs: Upper Body

arm	*el brazo*
	ehl BRAH-soh
armpit	*la axila*
	lah AHK-see-lah
biceps	*el bíceps*
	ehl BEE-sehps
elbow	*el codo*
	ehl KOH-doh
finger	*el dedo*
	ehl DEH-doh
forearm	*el antebrazo*
	ehl ahn-teh-BRAH-soh
hand	*la mano*
	lah MAH-noh
nail	*la uña*
	lah OO-nyah
thumb	*el pulgar*
	ehl pool-GAHR
wrist	*la muñeca*
	lah moo-NYEH-kah

The Limbs: Lower Body

ankle	*el tobillo*
	ehl toh-BEE-yoh
foot	*el pie*
	ehl pee-EH
heel	*el talón*
	ehl tah-LOHN
hip	*la cadera*
	lah kah-DEH-rah

knee	*la rodilla*
	lah roh-DEE-yah
leg	*la pierna*
	lah pee-YEHR-nah
shin	*la espinilla*
	lah eh-spee-NEE-yah
thigh	*el muslo*
	ehl MOOS-loh
toe	*el dedo del pie*
	ehl DEH-doh dehl pee-EH

Explain the Pain

As with most other subjects covered in this book, knowledge of a just a few basic verbs and the appropriate vocabulary terms will go a long way at the doctor's office. The verb *tener,* to have, (conjugated in Chapter 4) is useful when talking about your ailments. Here are some other verbs that'll come in handy:

- *examinar:* to examine
- *sentirse:* to feel (well, ill)
- *tener:* to have

EXAMINAR: to examine

yo examino (ehk-SAH-mee-noh)
tú examinas (ehk-SAH-mee-nahs)
él, ella, usted examina (ehk-SAH-mee-nah)
nosotros examinamos (ehk-sah-mee-NAH-mohs)

vosotros examináis (ehk-sah-mee-NAYHS)
ellos, ellas, ustedes examinan (ehk-SAH-mee-nahn)

El doctor examina al hombre herido.
The doctor examines the injured man.

Los científicos examinan el espécimen.
The scientists examine the specimen.

SENTIRSE: to feel (well, ill)

yo me siento (see-YEHN-toh)
tú te sientes (se-YEHN-tehs)
él, ella, usted se siente (see-YEHN-teh)
nosotros nos sentimos (sehn-TEE-mohs)
vosotros os sentís (sehn-TEES)
ellos, ellas, ustedes se sienten (see-YEHN-tehn)

Note that *sentirse* is a reflexive verb, so don't forget the object pronouns.

Me siento mal.
I don't feel well.

¿Cómo te sientes?
How do you feel?

Ahora que hemos comido, nos sentimos muy bien.
Now that we've eaten, we feel very well.

TENER: to have

yo tengo (TEHN-goh)
tú tienes (tee-EHN-ehs)
él, ella, usted tiene (tee-EHN-eh)
nosotros tenemos (teh-NEH-mohs)
vosotros tenéis (tehn-EHYS)
ellos, ellas, ustedes tienen (tee-EHN-ehn)

Tengo dolor de estómago.
My stomach hurts.

¿Tiene algunas preguntas?
Do you have any questions?

Los doctores tienen prisa.
The doctors are in a hurry.

 ALERT!

It's bad enough to be without your clothes when an airline loses your belongings, but imagine if your essential prescription medications were lost too. Prescriptions issued at home might not be that easy to refill abroad. To avoid the hassles, pack them in your carry-on luggage.

Common Ailments

allergy	*la alergia*
	lah ah-LEHR-hee-ah
allergic reaction	*la reacción alérgica*
	lah reh-ahk-see-OHN ah-LEHR-hee-kah
appendicitis	*la apendicitis*
	lah ah-pehn-dee-SEE-tees
arthritis	*la artritis*
	lah ahr-TREE-tees
asthma	*el asma*
	ehl AHS-mah
backache	*el dolor de espalda*
	el doh-LOHR deh eh-SPAHL-dah
bronchitis	*la bronquitis*
	lah brohn-KEE-tees
bruise	*la contusión*
	lah kohn-too-see-YOHN
burn	*la quemadura*
	lah keh-mah-DOO-rah
cancer	*el cáncer*
	ehl KAHN-sehr
cold	*el resfriado*
	ehl rehs-free-AH-doh
chest cold	*el catarro*
	ehl kah-TAH-rroh
head cold	*el constipado*
	ehl kohn-stee-PAH-doh
constipation	*el estreñimiento*
	ehl eh-streh-nyee-mee-EHN-toh

cough	*la tos*
	lah tohs
cut	*el corte*
	ehl KOHR-teh
dizziness	*el vértigo*
	ehl VEHR-tee-goh
to faint	*desmayarse*
	dehs-mah-YAHR-seh
flu	*la gripa*
	lah GREE-pah
heart attack	*el ataque al corazón*
	ehl ah-TAH-keh ahl koh-rah-SOHN
heartburn	*la acidez*
	lah ah-see-DEHS
indigestion	*la indigestión*
	lah een-dee-hehs-tee-OHN
infection	*la infección*
	lah een-fehk-see-OHN
insect bite	*la picadura de insecto*
	lah pee-kah-DOO-rah deh een-SEHK-toh
kidney stone	*el cálculo renal*
	ehl KAHL-koo-loh reh-NAHL
migraine	*la migraña*
	lah mee-GRAH-nyah
nosebleed	*la hemorragia nasal*
	lah eh-moh-RRAH-hee-ah nah-SAHL
pacemaker	*el marcapasos*
	ehl mahr-kah-PAH-sohs

Common Ailments (continued)

rash	*el sarpullido*
	ehl sahr-poo-YEE-doh
stroke	*apoplejía*
	ah-poh-pleh-HEE-ah
swelling	*la hinchazón*
	lah een-chah-SOHN
sunstroke	*la insolación*
	lah een-soh-lah-see-OHN
tetanus	*el tétano*
	ehl TEH-tah-noh
tonsilitis	*la amigdalitis*
	lah ah-meeg-dah-LEE-tees
toothache	*el dolor de muelas*
	ehl doh-LOHR deh MWEH-lahs
ulcer	*la úlcera*
	lah OOL-seh-rah
vomiting	*los vómitos*
	lohs VOH-mee-tohs
wound	*la herida*
	lah eh-REE-dah

In the Patient's Words

Did you forget that the rule about not drinking tap water also includes ice cubes? Spent a little too much time in the sun? Twisted your ankle running with the bulls? Here are some phrases you'll want to know to get the medical care you need.

My . . . hurts
Me duele . . .
meh DWEH-leh

I need an appointment with the doctor.
Necesito una cita con el doctor.
neh-seh-SEE-toh OO-nah SEE-tah kohn ehl dohk-TOHR

I have an appointment to see . . .
Tengo una cita para ver . . .
TEHN-goh OO-nah SEE-tah PAH-rah vehr

I'm dizzy.
Estoy mareado/a.
eh-STOHY mah-reh-AH-doh/dah

I'm nauseated.
Tengo náuseas.
TEHN-goh NOW-seh-ahs

I'm bleeding.
Estoy sangrando.
eh-STOHY sahn-GRAHN-doh

I don't feel well.
Me siento mal.
meh see-YEHN-toh mahl

I take medication for . . .
Tomo medicación para . . .
TOH-moh meh-dee-kah-see-OHN PAH-rah

I have a fever.
Tengo fiebre.
TEHN-goh fee-EH-breh

I've had a fever since . . .
Tengo fiebre desde . . .
TEHN-goh fee-EH-breh DEHS-deh

I'm pregnant.
Estoy embarazada.
eh-STOHY ehm-bah-rah-SAH-dah

I fell.
Me caí.
meh kah-EEH

I burned myself.
Me quemé.
meh keh-MEH

I had an accident.
Tuve un accidente.
TOO-veh oon ahk-see-DEHN-teh

I'm allergic to . . .
Soy alérgico/a a . . .
sohy ah-LEHR-hee-koh/kah ah

What the Doctor Might Say

If you want to understand what your doctor says—
or if you *are* the doctor—the following phrases will
come in handy.

How are you?
¿Cómo está?
KOH-moh eh-STAH

How do you feel today?
¿Cómo se siente hoy?
KOH-moh seh see-EHN-teh ohy

I am going to . . .
Voy a . . .
vohy ah

. . . draw a blood sample.
. . . *tomar una muestra de sangre.*
toh-MAHR OO-nah MWEH-strah deh SAHN-greh

. . . take your blood pressure.
. . . *tomarle la presión sanguínea.*
toh-MAHR-leh lah preh-see-OHN sahn-GHEE-neh-ah

. . . take your pulse.
. . . *tomarle el pulso.*
toh-MAHR-leh ehl POOL-soh

. . . listen to your heart.
. . . *auscultarle el corazón.*
ow-skool-TAHR-leh ehl koh-rah-SOHN

. . . check your reflexes.
. . . *comprobar los reflejos.*
kohm-proh-BAHR lohs reh-FLEH-hohs

Where does it hurt? / Show me.
¿Dónde le duele? / Muéstreme.
DOHN-deh leh DWEH-leh / MWEH-strah-meh

It's not serious.
No es grave.
noh ehs GRAH-veh

Do you have any allergies?
¿Tiene alguna alergia?
tee-EHN-eh ahl-GOO-nah ah-LEHR-hee-ah

Can you move your . . . ?
¿Puede mover el/la . . . ?
PWEH-deh moh-VEHR ehl/lah

Are you taking any medication?
¿Está tomando alguna medicación?
eh-STAH toh-MAHN-doh ahl-GOO-nah meh-dee-kah-see-OHN

How long have you felt this way?
¿Desde cuándo se siente así?
DEHS-deh KWAHN-doh seh see-EHN-teh ah-SEE

Chapter 12

The Local Community

S panish isn't just for travelers. You may be surprised by how many opportunities you have to use it in your own town, whether you're teaching bilingual students, going to the local market, or even making your way around your town.

At School

With greater numbers of Spanish-speaking children in schools each year, Spanish language skills can come in handy for teachers, students, and parents alike. To begin, here are a few verbs you might find helpful in a school setting:

- *aprender*: to learn
- *estudiar*: to study
- *enseñar*: to teach

 FACT

> If your child is studying Spanish in school, you can help by labeling household items in Spanish. All you need are some index cards and a roll of tape. It's more natural and effective to learn a language by associating vocabulary with an actual object, rather than trying to remember the English word and its translation.

APRENDER: to learn

yo aprendo (ah-PREHN-doh)
tú aprendes (ah-PREHN-dehs)
él, ella, usted aprende (ah-PREHN-deh)
nosotros aprendemos (ah-prehn-DEH-mohs)
vosotros aprendéis (ah-prehn-DEHYS)
ellos, ellas, ustedes aprenden (ah-PREHN-dehn)

Los niños aprenden mejor si no hay distracciones.
Children learn better without distractions.

Ella aprende rápidamente.
She learns quickly.

ESTUDIAR: to study

yo estudio (eh-STOO-dee-yoh)
tú estudias (eh-STOO-dee-yahs)
él, ella, usted estudia (eh-STOO-dee-yah)
nosotros estudiamos (eh-stoo-dee-YAH-mohs)
vosotros estudiáis (eh-stoo-dee-AH-ees)
ellos, ellas, ustedes estudian (eh-STOO-dee-yahn)

Estudiamos juntos.
We study together.

No estudian bastante.
They don't study enough.

Necesitas estudiar más.
You need to study more.

ENSEÑAR: to teach

yo enseño (ehn-SEHN-yoh)
tú enseñas (ehn-SEHN-yahs)
él, ella, usted enseña (ehn-SEHN-yah)
nosotros enseñamos (ehn-sehn-YAH-mohs)
vosotros enseñáis (ehn-sehn-YAHYS)
ellos, ellas, ustedes enseñan (ehn-SEHN-yahn)

El maestro enseña la clase.
The teacher teaches the class.

Mis padres me enseñan lo que es correcto.
My parents teach me what is right.

Now that you've got the verbs down, let's add some vocabulary and phrases. These might be used by the student's parent or the teacher.

 ESSENTIAL

While you're exploring the Spanish language, why not explore the cuisines of some Spanish-speaking countries as well? Supermarkets carry a wide selection of international food items these days, from tropical produce to exotic spices.

School Vocabulary

school	*la escuela*
	lah eh-SKWEH-lah
student	*el/la estudiante*
	ehl/lah eh-stoo-dee-AHN-teh
teacher	*el/la maestro/a*
	ehl/lah mah-YEH-stroh/ah
class	*la clase*
	lah KLAH-seh

grade	*el nivel*
	ehl nee-VEHL
principal	*el/la director/a*
	ehl/lah dee-rehk-TOHR/ah
classroom	*el aula*
	ehl OW-lah
desk	*el pupitre*
	ehl poo-PEE-treh
to graduate	*graduarse*
	grah-doo-AHR-seh
graduation	*la graduación*
	lah grah-doo-ah-see-OHN
diploma	*el diploma*
	ehl dee-PLOH-mah
book	*el libro*
	ehl LEE-broh
test	*la prueba*
	lah proo-EH-bah
to pass	*sacar una aprobación*
	sah-KAHR OON-ah ah-proh-bah-see-OHN
to fail	*reprobar*
	reh-proh-BAHR

Who is your child?
¿Quién es su hijo/a?
kee-EHN ehs soo EE-hoh/ah

My child's name is . . .
Mi hijo/a se llama . . .
mee EE-hoh/hah seh YAH-mah

I'm your child's teacher.
Soy el maestro/la maestra de su hijo/a.
sohy ehl mah-EH-stroh/lah mah-EH-strah deh soo EE-hoh/hah

Your child is doing well with . . .
Su hijo/a tiene éxito en . . .
soo EE-hoh/hah tee-EH-neh EHK-see-toh ehn

Your child is having problems with . . .
Su hijo/a tiene dificultades con . . .
soo EE-hoh/hah tee-EHN-eh dee-fee-kool-TAH-dehs kohn

Your child may need glasses.
Es posible que su hijo/a necesite gafas.
ehs poh-SEE-bleh keh soo EE-hoh/hah neh-seh-SEE-teh GAH-fahs

How is my child doing in class?
¿Cómo se porta mi hijo/a en clase?
KOH-moh seh POHR-tah mee EE-hoh/hah ehn KLAH-seh

 ALERT!

> If your children are learning Spanish, remind
> them to address all adults with *usted* unless
> the adult tells them otherwise!

At the Supermarket

Sure, your local supermarket probably hires workers who are fluent in English—unless, of course, you're doing your grocery shopping abroad. But there are sure to be Spanish-speaking employees as well. Why not grab your chance to practice your Spanish and ask them for help in their native language?

To start, here are the two verbs you are most likely to need:

* *comprar:* to buy
* *pagar:* to pay

COMPRAR: to buy

yo compro (KOHM-proh)
tú compras (KOHM-prahs)
él, ella, usted compra (KOHM-prah)
nosotros compramos (kohm-PRAH-mohs)
vosotros compráis (kohm-PRAHYS)
ellos, ellas, ustedes compran (KOHM-prahn)

Compro manzanas y naranjas en el supermercado.
I buy apples and oranges at the supermarket.

Compráis la comida a buen precio.
You buy dinner at a good price.

Hay que comprar comestibles.
I have to buy groceries.

PAGAR: to pay

yo pago (PAH-goh)
tú pagas (PAH-gahs)
él, ella, usted paga (PAH-gah)
nosotros pagamos (pah-GAH-mohs)
vosotros pagáis (pah-GAHYS)
ellos, ellas, ustedes pagan (PAH-gahn)

Ustedes pagan demasiado por el desayuno.
You pay too much for breakfast.

Pagas tus cuentas tarde.
You pay your bills late.

Supermarket Vocabulary

aisle	*el pasillo*
	ehl pah-SEE-yoh
cash	*el efectivo*
	ehl eh-fehk-TEE-voh
check	*el cheque*
	ehl CHEH-keh
credit card	*la tarjeta de crédito*
	lah tahr-HEH-tah deh KREH-dee-toh
cash register	*la caja*
	lah KAH-hah
shopping cart	*el carrito*
	ehl kah-RREE-toh
price	*el precio*
	ehl PREH-see-oh
paper bag	*la bolsa de papel*
	lah BOHL-sah deh pah-PEHL

plastic bag	*la bolsa de plástico*
	lah BOHL-sah deh PLAH-stee-koh
manager	*el/la gerente*
	ehl/lah heh-REHN-teh
fresh	*fresco*
	FREH-skoh
spoiled	*echado a perder*
	eh-CHAH-doh ah pehr-DEHR
on sale	*rebajado*
	reh-BAH-hah-doh
coupon	*el cupón*
	ehl koo-POHN
rebate	*el reembolso*
	ehl reh-ehm-BOHL-soh
supermarket	*el supermercado*
	ehl soo-pehr-mehr-KAH-doh

Where can I find . . . ?
¿Dónde puedo encontrar . . . ?
DOHN-deh PWEH-doh ehn-kohn-TRAHR

Can I write a personal check?
¿Puedo escribir un cheque personal?
PWEH-doh eh-skree-BEER oon CHEH-keh pehr-soh-NAHL

Can you check the price on this?
¿Puede chequear el precio de esto?
PWEH-deh cheh-keh-YAHR ehl PREH-see-yoh deh EH-stoh

I have a coupon.
Tengo un cupón.
TEHN-goh oon koo-POHN

Isn't that on sale?
¿No está rebajado esto?
noh eh-STAH reh-BAH-hah-doh EH-stoh

That's the wrong price.
Este precio es incorrecto.
EH-steh PREH-see-oh ehs een-koh-RREHK-toh

You gave me the wrong change.
Me dió el cambio incorrecto.
meh dee-OH ehl KAHM-bee-oh een-koh-RREHK-toh

Around Town

To end the chapter, here are a few general terms you might need as you make your way around town.

General Terms

building	*el edificio*
	ehl eh-dee-FEE-see-oh
park	*el parque*
	ehl PAHR-keh
bank	*el banco*
	ehl BAHN-koh
shopping mall	*el centro comercial*
	ehl SEHN-troh koh-mehr-see-AHL

street	*la calle*
	lah KAH-yeh
road	*el camino*
	ehl kah-MEE-noh
parking lot	*el aparcamiento*
	ehl ah-pahr-kah-mee-EHN-toh
sidewalk	*la acera*
	lah ah-SEH-rah
city hall	*el ayuntamiento*
	ehl ah-yuhn-tah-mee-EHN-toh
courthouse	*el palacio de justicia*
	ehl pah-LAH-see-yoh deh hoo-STEE-see-ah
jail	*la cárcel*
	lah KAHR-sehl
police station	*la comisaría*
	lah koh-mee-sah-REE-ah
hospital	*el hospital*
	ehl ohs-pee-TAHL
post office	*la oficina de correos*
	lah oh-fee-SEE-nah deh koh-RREH-ohs
mayor	*el alcalde/la alcadesa*
	ehl ahl-KAHL-deh/lah ahl-kah-DEH-sah
judge	*el juez/la jueza*
	ehl hwehs/lah HWEH-sah
police officer	*el/la policía*
	ehl/lah poh-lee-SEE-ah
postal worker	*el/la cartero/a*
	ehl/lah kahr-TEH-roh/rah

General Terms (continued)

mailbox *el buzón*
ehl boo-SOHN

neighbor *el/la vecino/a*
ehl/lah beh-SEE-noh/nah

Tempted to hum a few bars of "It's a Small World" now? Go right ahead. It's true.

 ALERT!

Will raising children in a bilingual household delay their language skills?
Studies have found this is not the case. In fact, bilingual children develop additional neural pathways in their brains. They were found to be better at math and science later in life.

Chapter 13
Spanish at Home

Why on earth would you need to use Spanish in your own English-speaking home? Well, you might host a Spanish-speaking exchange student for a semester. Or you may employ someone in the household who's more comfortable speaking Spanish. Or maybe you think it would make family build-your-own-burrito nights a bit more interesting! Whatever your reason, you'll find the phrases and vocabulary terms in this chapter to get you chatting *pronto*.

Things to Do at Home

So far you've learned a lot of verbs for when you're out and about traveling, shopping, or working. Here are some everyday verbs for the things you and your family do at home.

- *cocinar:* to cook
- *descansar:* to rest
- *dormir:* to sleep
- *jugar:* to play

COCINAR: to cook

yo cocino (koh-SEE-noh)
tú cocinas (koh-SEE-nahs)
él, ella, usted cocina (koh-SEE-nah)
nosotros cocinamos (koh-see-NAH-mohs)
vosotros cocináis (koh-see-NAHYS)
ellos, ellas, ustedes cocinan (koh-SEE-nahn)

Yo cocino espinacas con ajo.
I cook spinach with garlic.

Mario cocina el desayuno los sábados.
Mario cooks breakfast every Saturday.

Ramona y Oswald cocinan de vez en cuando.
Ramona and Oswald cook once in a while.

DESCANSAR: to rest

yo descanso (dehs-KAHN-soh)
tú descansas (dehs-KAHN-sahs)
él, ella, usted descansa (dehs-KAHN-sah)
nosotros descansamos (dehs-kahn-SAH-mohs)
vosotros descansáis (dehs-kahn-SAHYS)
ellos, ellas, ustedes descansan (dehs-KAHN-sahn)

Mi abuela descansa en el sofá.
My grandmother rests on the couch.

Descansamos los domingos.
We rest on Sundays.

¿Por qúe no descansas un ratito?
Why don't you rest for a little bit?

DORMIR: to sleep

yo duermo (DWEHR-moh)
tú duermes (DWEHR-mehs)
él, ella, usted duerme (DWEHR-meh)
nosotros dormimos (dohr-MEE-mohs)
vosotros dormís (dohr-MEES)
ellos, ellas, ustedes duermen (DWEHR-mehn)

Mi marido duerme boca arriba.
My husband sleeps on his back.

Ellos duermen la siesta.
They take a siesta.

Tú duermes a pierna suelta.
You sleep like a log.

 FACT

> There are a number of words in Spanish for bedroom, including *cuarto de dormir*, *habitación, dormitorio*, and *recámara*. Each one is popular in particular regions, but any one will get you understood.

JUGAR: to play

yo juego (HWEH-goh)
tú juegas (HWEH-gahs)
él, ella, usted juega (HWEH-gah)
nosotros jugamos (hoo-GAH-mohs)
vosotros jugáis (hoo-GAHYS)
ellos, ellas, ustedes juegan (HWEH-gahn)

Juego al tenis con mi hermano.
I play tennis with my brother.

Juegan a los naipes cada sábado a la medianoche.
They play cards every Saturday at midnight.

¿Quieres jugar un juego?
Want to play a game?

Note that the verb *jugar* is used to talk about playing a game or sport. It is not used to talk about playing a musical instrument. In that instance you would use the verb *tocar,* to touch. *Jugar* is also not used in many of the idiomatic ways "to play" is used in English. For example, you would not use *jugar* to say, "play a role," "play it safe," or "play dead." See Chapter 14 for these and other idiomatic phrases.

The Anatomy of a House

From the basement to the attic, here are the terms you can use if you are speaking Spanish.

From Basement to Attic

attic	*el desván*
	ehl dehs-VAHN
backyard	*el jardín*
	ehl hahr-DEEN
basement	*el sótano*
	ehl SOH-tah-noh
bathroom	*el cuarto de baño*
	ehl KWAHR-to deh BAH-nyoh
bedroom	*la habitación*
	lah ah-bee-tah-see-OHN
ceiling	*el techo*
	ehl TEH-choh

From Basement to Attic (continued)

closet	*el armario*
	ehl ahr-MAH-ree-oh
dining room	*el comedor*
	ehl koh-meh-DOHR
driveway	*el camino de entrada*
	ehl kah-MEE-noh deh ehn-TRAH-dah
family room	*la sala de estar*
	lah SAH-lah de eh-STAHR
floor	*el suelo*
	ehl SWEH-loh
floor (level, story)	*el piso*
	ehl PEE-soh
garage	*el garaje*
	ehl gah-RAH-heh
guest room	*el cuarto de los invitados*
	ehl KWAHR-toh deh lohs een-vee-TAH-dohs
kitchen	*la cocina*
	lah koh-SEE-nah
living room	*la sala*
	lah SAH-lah
master bedroom	*el dormitorio principal*
	ehl dohr-mee-TOH-ree-oh preen-see-PAHL
nursery	*el cuarto de los niños*
	ehl KWAHR-toh deh lohs NEE-nyohs
patio	*el patio*
	ehl PAH-tee-oh
powder room	*el tocador*
	ehl toh-kah-DOHR

roof	*el tejado*
	ehl teh-HAH-doh
room	*el cuarto*
	ehl KWAHR-toh
wall	*la pared*
	lah pah-REHD

Everything Near the Kitchen Sink

blender	*la licuadora*
	lah lee-kwah-DOH-rah
cabinet	*el armario de cocina*
	ehl ahr-MAH-ree-oh deh koh-SEE-nah
dishtowel	*el trapo de fregar*
	ehl TRAH-poh deh freh-GAHR
dishwasher	*el lavaplatos*
	ehl lah-vah-PLAH-tohs
drawer	*el cajón*
	ehl kah-HON
freezer	*el congelador*
	ehl kohn-heh-lah-DOHR
garbage can	*el cubo de la basura*
	ehl KOO-boh deh lah bah-SOO-rah
kitchen sink	*el fregadero*
	ehl freh-gah-DEH-roh
microwave	*el microondas*
	ehl mee-kro-OHN-dahs
oven	*el horno*
	ehl OHR-noh
pan	*la sartén*
	lah sahr-TEHN

Everything Near the Kitchen Sink (continued)

pantry	*la despensa*
	lah dehs-PEHN-sah
paper towel	*la toalla de papel*
	lah toh-AH-yah deh pah-PEHL
plastic bag	*la bolsa de plástico*
	lah BOHL-sah deh PLAH-stee-koh
pot	*la olla*
	lah OHY-yah
refrigerator	*la nevera*
	lah neh-BEH-rah
roach	*la cucaracha*
	lah koo-kah-RAH-chah
stove	*la estufa*
	lah eh-STOO-fah
toaster	*la tostadora*
	lah toh-stah-DOH-rah

The Family Room

board game	*el juego de mesa*
	ehl HWEH-goh deh MEH-sah
cable TV	*la televisión por cable*
	lah teh-leh-vee-see-YOHN pohr KAH-bleh
CD player	*el tocador de discos compactos*
	ehl toh-kah-DOHR deh DEES-kohs kohm-PAHK-tohs
compact disc	*el disco compacto*
	ehl DEES-koh kohm-PAHK-toh

couch	*el sofá*
	ehl soh-FAH
easy chair	*el butacón*
	ehl boo-tah-KOHN
mess	*el desorden*
	ehl dehs-OHR-dehn
remote control	*el control remoto*
	ehl KOHN-trol reh-MOH-toh
stereo	*el estéreo*
	ehl eh-STEH-reh-oh
television	*la televisión*
	OO-nah teh-leh-vee-see-YOHN
toy	*el juguete*
	ehl hoo-GEH-teh
VCR	*el grabador de video*
	ehl grah-bah-DOHR deh vee-DEH-yoh
videotape	*la videocinta*
	lah vee-deh-yoh SEEN-tah

 FACT

Jugar is found in a lot of idiomatic phrases. For example: *jugar con fuego* (to play with fire) and *jugársela* (to take a chance—review reflexive verbs for this one).

In the Bedroom

alarm clock	*el despertador*
	ehl dehs-pehr-tah-DOHR
bed	*la cama*
	lah KAH-mah
blanket	*la manta*
	lah MAHN-tah
bureau	*la cómoda*
	lah KOH-moh-dah
closet	*el armario*
	ehl ahr-MAH-ree-oh
curtain	*la cortina*
	lah kohr-TEE-nah
drawer	*el cajón*
	ehl kah-HOHN
dresser	*el tocador*
	ehl toh-kah-DOHR
headboard	*la cabecera*
	lah kah-beh-SEH-rah
lamp	*la lámpara*
	lah LAHM-pah-rah
mirror	*el espejo*
	ehl eh-SPEH-hoh
nightlight	*la lamparilla*
	lah lahm-pah-REE-yah
pillow	*la almohada*
	lah ahl-moh-AH-dah
sheet	*la sábana*
	lah SAH-bah-nah

In the Bathroom

bathroom sink	*el lavabo*
	ehl lah-VAH-boh
bathtub	*la bañera*
	lah bah-NYEH-rah
bathmat	*la alfombra de baño*
	lah ahl-FOHM-brah deh BAH-nyoh
bidet	*un bidé*
	oon bee-DEH
conditioner	*la crema suavizante*
	lah KREH-mah swah-vee-SAHN-teh
mold	*el moho*
	ehl MOH-hoh
razor	*la navaja de afeitar*
	lah nah-VAH-hah deh ah-fehy-TAHR
rubber ducky	*el pato de goma*
	ehl PAH-toh deh GOH-mah
shampoo	*el champú*
	ehl chahm-POO
shower	*la ducha*
	lah DOO-chah
soap	*el jabón*
	ehl hah-BOHN
toilet	*el retrete*
	ehl reh-TREH-teh
toothpaste	*el dentífrico*
	ehl dehn-TEE-free-koh
towel	*la toalla*
	lah toh-AY-yah
washcloth	*la manopla*
	lah mah-NOH-plah

In the Garden

birdbath	*la pila para pájaros*
	lah PEE-lah PAH-rah PAH-hah-rohs
bat	*el murciélago*
	ehl moor-see-EH-lah-goh
beetle	*el escarabajo*
	ehl ehs-kah-rah-BAH-hoh
bush	*el arbusto*
	ehl ahr-BOOS-toh
cicada	*la cigarra*
	lah see-GAH-rrah
cricket	*el grillo*
	ehl GREE-yoh
dragonfly	*la libélula*
	lah lee-BEH-loo-lah
fence	*la cerca*
	lah SEHR-kah
flower	*la flor*
	lah flohr
grass (lawn)	*el césped*
	ehl SEHS-pehd
grasshopper	*el saltamontes*
	ehl sahl-tah-MOHN-tehs
grill	*la parrilla*
	lah pah-RREE-yah
grub	*la larva*
	lah LAHR-bah
hole	*el hoyo*
	ehl OHY-yoh

hose	*la manguera*
	lah mahn-GWEH-rah
ladybug	*la mariquita*
	lah mah-ree-KEE-tah
lawnmower	*el cortacéspedes*
	ehl kohr-tah-SEHS-peh-dehs
root	*la raíz*
	lah rah-EES
sapling	*el árbol joven*
	ehl AHR-bohl HOH-vehn
shrub	*el arbusto*
	ehl ahr-BOOS-toh
spider	*la araña*
	lah ah-RAH-nyah
sprinkler	*el aspersor*
	ehl ahs-pehr-SOHR
tree	*el árbol*
	ehl AHR-bohl
weed	*la mala hierba*
	lah MAH-lah ee-EHR-bah
worm	*el gusano*
	ehl goo-SAH-noh

In the Garage

bicycle	*la bicicleta*
	lah bee-see-KLEH-tah
bike	*la bici*
	lah BEE-see
car	*el coche*
	ehl KOH-cheh

In the Garage (continued)

garbage can	*el cubo de basura*
	ehl KOO-boh deh bah-SOO-rah
moped	*el ciclomotor*
	ehl see-kloh moh-TOHR
motorcycle	*la motocicleta*
	lah moh-toh-see-KLEH-tah
scooter	*el escúter*
	ehl eh-SKOO-tehr
skateboard	*la patineta*
	lah pah-tee-NEH-tah
tool	*la herramienta*
	lah heh-rrah-mee-YEHN-tah
workbench	*el banco de trabajo*
	ehl BAHN-koh deh trah-BAH-hoh

In the Basement

boiler	*la caldera*
	lah kahl-DEH-rah
circuit breaker	*el cortacircuitos*
	ehl kohrta-seer-KWEE-tohs
clothes dryer	*la secadora*
	lah seh-kah-DOH-rah
furnace	*el horno*
	ehl OHR-noh
fuse box	*la caja de fusibles*
	lah KAH-hah deh foo-SEE-blehs
washer	*la lavadora*
	lah lah-vah-DOH-rah

Congratulations! You've made it through the main subject areas. All that's left ahead of you is a chapter on idioms and slang.

 ESSENTIAL

While you're watching *la televisión por cable*, why not switch to a Spanish-language channel for a while? It's a great way to build vocabulary and comprehension skills.

Chapter 14

Idioms, Sayings, and Slang

I dioms, sayings, and slang are those words and phrases that give a language its personality and color. Because they usually don't make sense when translated literally, you'll need to memorize them. Pick up one or two here, another three over there, until you have an impressive collection. Here's where you get to break the rules and have fun with language. For several sections of this chapter, the Spanish phrases are presented first. As a challenge, why not try to figure out the meaning of the Spanish phrase before you read the English translation?

Common Idioms

Idioms are words and phrases used in such a way that you can't decipher the whole by identifying the parts. They aren't something you can string together word-by-word from a dictionary. For example, imagine you were learning to speak English and you came across the phrase "The cat got her tongue." This idiom certainly can't be translated word for word. Instead, you would be taught what the idiom means as a whole.

Idiomatic Verb Phrases

acabar de ah-kah-BAHR deh	to have just
contar con kohn-TAHR kohn	to rely on
dar con dahr kohn	to find
dar en dahr ehn	to hit against
dar gritos dahr GREE-tohs	to shout
dar la bienvenida dahr lah bee-ehn-veh-NEE-dah	to welcome
dar un paseo dahr oon pah-SEH-oh	to take a walk
darse cuenta de DAHR-seh KWEHN-tah deh	to realize
darse por DAHR-seh pohr	to consider oneself

es decir ehs deh-SEER	that is to say
está bien eh-STAH bee-EHN	okay
estar bien eh-STAHR bee-EHN	to be well
estar mal eh-STAHR mahl	to be bad (ill)
estar a punto de + infinitive eh-STAHR ah POON-toh deh	to be about to
estar de acuerdo eh-STAHR deh ah-KWEHR-doh	to agree
estar de pie eh-STAHR deh pee-EH	to be standing
estar de vuelta eh-STAHR deh VWEHL-tah	to have returned
estar por eh-STAHR pohr	to be in favor of
hace buen tiempo AH-seh bwehn tee-EHM-poh	the weather is good
hace mal tiempo AH-seh mahl tee-EHM-poh	the weather is bad
hace calor AH-seh kah-LOHR	it's hot
hace frío AH-seh FREE-oh	it's cold
hace fresco AH-seh FREH-skoh	it's cool
hace sol AH-seh sohl	it's sunny

Idiomatic Verb Phrases (continued)

hace viento AH-seh vee-EHN-toh	it's windy
hacer una broma ah-SEHR OO-nah BROH-mah	to make a joke
hacer el papel de ah-SEHR ehl pah-PEHL deh	to play the role of
hacer una pregunta ah-SEHR OO-nah preh-GOON-tah	to ask a question
hacer un viaje ah-SEHR oon bee-YAH-heh	to take a trip
hacerse daño ah-SEHR-seh DAH-nyoh	to harm oneself
intentar de een-tehn-TAHR deh	to attempt
llegar a ser yeh-GAHR ah sehr	to become
poner en claro poh-NEHR ehn KLAH-roh	to make clear
poner en duda poh-NEHR ehn DOO-dah	to question
poner en marcha poh-NEHR ehn MAHR-chah	to set in motion
poner en ridículo poh-NEHR ehn ree-DEE-koo-loh	to make fun of
ponerse de acuerdo poh-NEHR-seh deh ah-KWEHR-doh	to reach an agreement
prestar atención preh-STAHR ah-tehn-see-OHN	to pay attention
querer decir keh-REHR deh-SEER	to mean

ser aficionado de	to be a fan of
sehr ah-fee-see-oh-NAH-doh deh	
ser de	to belong to
sehr deh	
tener . . . años	to be . . . years old
teh-NEHR . . . AH-nyohs	
tener calor	to be hot
teh-NEHR kah-LOHR	
tener frío	to be cold
teh-NEHR FREE-oh	
tener hambre	to be hungry
teh-NEHR AHM-breh	
tener sed	to be thirsty
teh-NEHR sehd	
tener éxito	to succeed
teh-NEHR EHK-see-toh	
tener razón	to be right
teh-NEHR rah-SOHN	
tener sueño	to be tired
teh-NEHR SWEH-nyoh	
tener cuidado	to be careful
teh-NEHR kwee-DAH-doh	
tener que ver con	to have to do with
teh-NEHR keh vehr kohn	
tener lugar	to take place
teh-NEHR loo-GAHR	
tener prisa	to be in a hurry
teh-NEHR PREE-sah	
tener miedo	to be afraid
teh-NEHR mee-EH-doh	

Idiomatic Verb Phrases (continued)

tener que + infinitive teh-NEHR keh	to have to
tratar de + infinitive trah-TAHR deh	to try to
valer la pena vah-LEHR lah PEH-nah	to be worth it

 FACT

Idioms and slang can bring any language to life. We each speak in ways very particular to ourselves. Experiment with these phrases and find the manner of speaking Spanish that best expresses who you are.

Other Idiomatic Phrases

absolutely	*por supuesto* pohr soo-PWEH-stoh
to add fuel to the fire	*echar leña al fuego* eh-CHAHR LEH-nyah ahl FWEH-goh
all of a sudden	*de repente* deh reh-PEHN-teh
Are you serious?	*¿En serio?* ehn SEH-ree-oh
at last	*por fin* pohr feen

at least	*por lo menos*
	pohr loh MEH-nohs
to be a great person	*ser buena gente*
	sehr BWEH-nah HEHN-teh
to be able to deal with	*poder con*
	poh-DEHR kohn
to be able to tell that	*se nota que*
	seh NOH-tah keh
to be mean	*ser una mula*
	sehr OO-nah MOO-lah
to be on everyone's lips	*andar de boca en boca*
	ahn-DAHR deh BOH-kah ehn BOH-kah
to be on your way	*estar en camino*
	eh-STAHR ehn kah-MEE-noh
to be ill	*sentirse mal*
	sehn-TEER-seh mahl
Be quiet!	*¡Cállate!*
	KAHY-yah-teh
to beat around the bush	*andarse con rodeos*
	ahn-DAHR-seh kohn roh-DEH-ohs
by the way	*a propósito*
	ah proh-POH-see-toh
carelessly	*al aventón*
	ahl ah-vehn-TOHN
to end up	*terminar en*
	tehr-mee-NAHR ehn
Enough already!	*¡Basta ya!*
	BAH-stah yah

Other Idiomatic Phrases (continued)

in the middle of	*a mediados de*
	ah meh-dee-AH-dohs deh
face up	*boca arriba*
	BOH-kah ah-RREE-bah
face down	*boca abajo*
	BOH-kah ah-BAH-hoh
to fall in love	*enamorarse de*
	eh-nah-moh-RAHR-seh deh
to feel like, to crave	*tener ganas de*
	teh-NEHR GAH-nahs deh
to feel sorry for	*sentir lástima por*
	sehn-TEEHR LAH-stee-mah pohr
first of all	*antes que nada*
	AHN-tehs keh NAH-dah
for good	*para siempre*
	PAH-rah see-EHM-preh
to get along with	*llevarse bien con (alguien)*
	yeh-BAHR-seh bee-YEHN kohn
	(AHL-gee-yehn)
to get up on the wrong	*levantarse con el pie izquierdo*
side of the bed	leh-vahn-TAHR-seh kohn ehl
	pee-EH ees-kee-EHR-doh
to give a hand to	*dar una mano a*
	dahr OO-nah MAH-noh ah
to go crazy	*volverse loco/a*
	vohl-VEHR-seh LOH-koh/kah
to go to great lengths	*mover cielo, mar y tierra*
	moh-VEHR see-EH-loh mahr ee
	tee-EH-rrah

to have a good time	*pasar bien*
	pah-SAHR bee-EHN
in the long run	*a la larga*
	ah lah LAHR-gah
in the meantime	*mientras tanto*
	mee-EHN-trahs TAHN-toh
luckily	*menos mal*
	MEH-nohs mahl
just what I needed	*lo que faltaba*
(sarcastic)	loh keh fahl-TAH-bah
to not be a big deal	*no ser para tanto*
	no sehr PAH-rah TAHN-toh
once in a while	*de vez en cuando*
	deh vehs ehn KWAHN-doh
one thing after another	*llover sobre mojado*
	yoh-VEHR SOH-breh moh-HAH-doh
to rain cats and dogs	*llover a cántaros*
	yoh-VEHR ah KAHN-tah-rohs
to scare	*pegar un susto*
	peh-GAHR oon SOO-stoh

Say It with a Saying

Sayings, or *refranes* (reh-FRAH-nehs), are a big part of the spoken Spanish language. Each country and culture has their own, but many cross the borders and are embraced by Spanish speakers worldwide. These *refranes* are so old that most of those who use them would be hard-pressed to tell you how they originated.

Remember, the translations given provide the meaning of the saying; for the most part, they aren't literal.

A caballo regalado no le mires los dientes.
Don't look a gift horse in the mouth.
ah kah-BAH-yoh reh-gah-LAH-doh noh leh MEE-rehs lohs dee-EHN-tehs

A donde el corazón se inclina, el pie camina.
Home is where the heart is.
ah DOHN-deh ehl koh-rah-SOHN seh een-KLEE-nah ehl pee-EH kah-MEE-nah

A mucha hambre, no hay pan duro.
Beggars can't be choosers.
ah MOO-chah HAM-breh noh ahy pahn DOO-roh

A rey muerto, rey puesto.
When one door closes, another opens.
ah rehy MWEHR-toh rehy PWEH-stoh

Algo es algo.
It's better than nothing.
AHL-goh ehs AHL-goh

Con paciencia y con maña, el elefante se comió la araña.
Small strokes fell great oaks.
kohn pah-see-EHN-see-ah ee kohn MAH-nyah ehl eh-leh-FAHN-teh seh koh-mee-OH lah ah-RAH-nyah

Dime con quién andas y te diré quién eres.
Tell me who your friends are and I'll tell you who you are.
DEE-meh kohn kee-EHN AHN-dahs ee teh dee-REH kee-EHN EH-rehs

Donde hay humo, hay calor.
Where there's smoke, there's fire.
DOHN-deh ahy OO-moh ahy KAH-lohr

Lo barato sale caro.
Cheap things cost you in the end.
loh bah-RAH-toh SAH-leh KAH-roh

El mundo es un pañuelo.
It's a small world.
ehl MOON-doh ehs oon pah-nyoo-EH-loh

El tiempo da buen consejo.
Time will tell.
ehl tee-EHM-poh dah bwehn kohn-SEH-hoh

Las penas con pan son menos.
Grief is lessened with bread.
lahs PEH-nahs kohn pahn sohn MEH-nohs

No hay dos sin tres.
Bad (good) things come in threes.
noh ahy dohs seen trehs

No hay moros en la costa.
The coast is clear.
noh ahy MOH-rohs ehn lah KOH-stah

No hay pero que valga.
No ands, ifs or buts.
noh ahy PEH-roh keh VAHL-gah

No todo es miel sobre hojuelas.
It's not all fun and games.
noh TOH-doh ehs mee-EHL SOH-breh oh-HWEH-lahs

Querer es poder.
Where there's a will, there's a way.
keh-REHR ehs poh-DEHR

Ver para creer.
Seeing is believing.
behr PAH-rah kreh-EHR

 ESSENTIAL

> *Tener que* + infinitive is an extremely useful idiomatic verb phrase. Use it to express what you have to do. For example: *tengo que trabajar*—I have to work.

Words Your Spanish Teacher Never Taught You

Learning slang in a foreign language is a lot of fun and can add flavor to your conversation skills. Just as in English, though, be sure you know when to use it and when more formal language is appropriate. As always, when in doubt, it's best to err on the side of formality.

First, try these slang verbs on for size. Yes, they still have to be conjugated. *No todo es miel sobre hojuelas,* after all.

- *cabecear:* to nod off while sitting up
- *codearse:* to rub shoulders with
- *jalarse*: to get drunk
- *jorobar*: to pester
- *meterse con*: to mess with, to get involved with
- *paluchear*: to pretend to be something you're not, to pose

CABECEAR: to nod off while sitting up

yo cabeceo (kah-beh-SEH-oh)
tú cabeceas (kah-beh-SEH-ahs)
él, ella, usted cabecea (kah-beh-SEH-ah)
nosotros cabeceamos (kah-beh-seh-AH-mohs)
vosotros cabeceáis (kah-beh-seh-AHYS)
ellos, ellas, ustedes cabecean (kah-beh-SEH-ahn)

Cabeceamos en la clase de matemática.
We nod off in math class.

JALARSE: to get drunk

yo me jaleo (hah-LEH-oh)
tú te jaleas (hah-LEH-ahs)
él, ella, usted se jalea (hah-LEH-ah)
nosotros nos jaleamos (hah-leh-AH-mohs)
vosotros os jaleáis (hah-leh-AHYS)
ellos, ellas, ustedes se jalean (hah-LEH-ahn)

Los amigos se jalean en la fiesta.
The friends get drunk at the party.

JOROBAR: to pester

yo jorobo (hoh-ROH-boh)
tú jorobas (hoh-ROH-bahs)
él, ella, usted joroba (hoh-ROH-bah)
nosotros jorobamos (hoh-roh-BAH-mohs)
vosotros jorobáis (hoh-roh-BAHYS)
ellos, ellas, ustedes joroban (hoh-ROH-bahn)

Mis hermanos pequeños me joroban sin piedad.
My little brothers pester me mercilessly.

METERSE CON: to mess with, to get involved with

yo me meto (MEH-toh)
tú te metes (MEH-tehs)
él, ella, usted se mete (MEH-teh)
nosotros nos metemos (meh-TEH-mohs)
vosotros os metéis (meh-TEHYS)
ellos, ellas, ustedes se meten (MEH-tehn)

No me meto con descarados.
I don't mess with scoundrels.

PALUCHEAR: to pretend to be something you're not, to pose

yo palucheo (pah-loo-CHEH-oh)
tú palucheas (pah-loo-CHEH-ahs)
él, ella, usted paluchea (pah-loo-CHEH-ah)
nosotros palucheamos (pah-loo-cheh-AH-mohs)
vosotros palucheáis (pah-loo-cheh-AHYS)
ellos, ellas, ustedes paluchean (pah-loo-CHEH-ahn)

Andrea paluchea como si fuera famosa.
Andrea acts like she's famous.

Slang Words and Phrases

a load of bull	*rollo*
	ROH-yoh
a lot	*un resto*
	oon REH-stoh
as is	*tal cual*
	tahl kwahl
to ask for trouble	*sacar boleto*
	sah-KAHR boh-LEH-toh
bad luck	*mala pata*
	MAH-lah PAH-tah
burn the midnight oil	*quemarse las pestañas*
	keh-MAHR-seh lahs peh-STAH-nyahs

Slang Words and Phrases (continued)

to brag	*darse bomba*
	DAHR-seh BOHM-bah
carelessly	*a la fresca viruta*
	ah lah FREH-skah vee-ROO-tah
Cool!	*¡Qué guay! ¡Qué padre!*
	keh gwahy/keh PAH-dreh
to give the creeps	*dar cosa a*
	dahr KOH-sah ah
Go to hell!	*¡Vete al diablo!*
	VEH-teh ahl dee-AH-bloh
It's all the same to me.	*Me da igual.*
	meh dah ee-GWAHL
to make a mistake	*pelar rata*
	peh-LAHR RAH-tah
Not a chance!	*¡Ni de chiste!*
	nee deh CHEEH-steh
okay, sure	*vale*
	VAH-leh
to paint the town red	*rumbiar*
	room-bee-AHR
so far, so good	*vamos bien*
	VAH-mohs bee-EHN
stupidly	*a lo idiota*
	ah loh ee-dee-OH-tah

Appendix A
Essential Words and Phrases

In too much of a hurry to flip through an entire chapter? Here are some of the most essential words and phrases. If you don't find what you're looking for here, refer back to the thematic chapters, check the dictionaries in Appendix B and C, or use the index.

Communicating

Please repeat.
Repita, por favor.
reh-PEE-tah pohr-fah-BOHR

Please speak more slowly.
Hable más despacio, por favor.
HAH-bleh mahs dehs-PAH-see-oh pohr fah-VOHR

Do you speak English?
¿Habla usted inglés?
AH-blah OO-stehd een-GLEHS

I don't understand.
No comprendo.
noh kohm-PREHN-doh

Eating Out

May I see a menu?
¿Puedo ver la carta?
PWEH-do vehr lah KAHR-tah

Do I need a reservation?
¿Necesito una reservación?
neh-seh-SEE-toh OO-nah rehs-ehr-vah-see-OHN

How is this prepared?
¿Cómo se prepara esto?
KOH-moh seh preh-PAH-rah EH-stoh

What do you recommend?
¿Qué recomienda usted?
keh reh-koh-mee-EHN-dah OO-stehd

What is this?
¿Qué es esto?
keh ehs EH-stoh

I'm a vegetarian.
Soy vegetariano/a.
sohy veh-heh-tah-ree-AH-noh/nah

I'm on a diet.
Estoy a régimen.
eh-STOHY ah REH-hee-mehn

I can't have . . .
No puedo tomar/comer . . .
noh PWEH-doh toh-MAHR/coh-MEHR

I'm allergic to . . .
Soy alérgico/a a . . .
sohy ah-LEHR-hee-koh/kah ah

In Case of an Emergency

emergency exit	*la salida de emergencia* lah sah-LEE-dah deh eh-mehr-HEN-see-ah
life vest	*el chaleco salvavidas* ehl chah-LEH-koh sahl-vah-VEE-dahs

In Case of an Emergency (continued)

allergy	*la alergia*
	lah ah-LEHR-hee-ah
allergic reaction	*la reacción alérgica*
	lah reh-ahk-see-OHN ah-LEHR-hee-kah
heart attack	*el ataque al corazón*
	ehl ah-TAH-keh ahl koh-rah-SOHN
pacemaker	*el marcapasos*
	ehl mahr-kah-PAH-sohs
stroke	*el ataque de apoplejía*
	ehl ah-TAH-keh deh ah-poh-pleh-HEE-ah
vomiting	*los vómitos*
	lohs VOH-mee-tohs

My . . . hurts
Me duele . . .
meh DWEH-leh

I need a doctor.
Necesito un doctor.
neh-seh-SEE-toh oon dohk-TOHR

I don't feel well.
Me siento mal.
meh see-EHN-toh mahl

I take medication for . . .
Tomo medicación para . . .
TOH-moh meh-dee-kah-see-OHN PAH-rah

Greetings

Hello	*Hola*
	OH-lah
Good morning	*Buenos días*
	BWEH-nos DEE-ahs
Good afternoon	*Buenas tardes*
	BWEH-nas TAHR-dehs
Good evening	*Buenas noches*
	BWEH-nas NOH-ches
My name is . . .	*Me llamo . . .*
	me YAH-mo
I am from . . .	*Soy de . . .*
	soy deh
good-bye	*adiós*
	ah-dee-OHS

Official Business

form of identification	*la forma de identificación*
	lah FOHR-mah deh ee-dehn-tee-fee-kah-see-OHN
passport	*el pasaporte*
	ehl pah-sah-POHR-teh
money	*el dinero*
	ehl dee-NEH-roh
cash	*el efectivo*
	ehl eh-fehk-TEE-voh
check	*el cheque*
	ehl CHEH-keh

Getting Around

Where is . . . ?
¿Dónde está . . . ?
DOHN-deh eh-STAH

I'm going to . . .
Voy a . . .
vohy ah

How do I get to . . . from here?
¿Cómo voy a . . . de aquí?
KOH-moh vohy ah . . . deh ah-KEE

Where is the American Embassy?
¿Dónde está la embajada americana?
DOHN-de eh-STAH lah ehm-bah-HAH-dah ah-meh-ree-KAH-nah

Where is the nearest bus stop?
¿Dónde está la parada de autobús más cercana?
DOHN-de eh-STAH lah pah-RAH-dah deh ow-toh-BOOS mahs sehr-KAH-nah

Where is the nearest metro station?
¿Dónde está la estación de metro más cercana?
DOHN-deh eh-STAH lah ehs-tah-see-OHN deh MEH-troh mahs sehr-KAH-nah

Can you show it to me on this map?
¿Puede enseñármelo en este mapa?
PWEH-deh ehn-sehn-YAHR-meh-loh ehn EH-steh MAH-pah

I'm lost.
Estoy perdido/a.
eh-STOHY pehr-DEE-doh/dah

General Questions

Where are the restrooms?
¿Dónde están los baños?
DOHN-deh ehs-TAHN lohs BAH-nyohs

What time is it?
¿Qué hora es?
keh OH-rah ehs

Can I have the bill, please?
¿Puedo tener la cuenta, por favor?
PWEH-doh teh-NEHR lah KWEHN-tah pohr fah-VOHR

Can you help me, please?
¿Puede usted ayudarme, por favor?
PWEH-deh OO-stehd ah-yoo-DAHR-meh pohr fah-VOHR

How much do I owe you?
¿Cuánto le debo?
KWAHN-toh leh DEH-boh

General Questions (continued)

Could you please . . . ?
¿Podría usted . . . , por favor?
poh-DREE-ah OO-stehd . . . pohr fah-VOHR

Could you give me . . . ?
¿Podría darme . . . ?
poh-DREE-ah DAHR-meh

Where can I find . . . ?
¿Dónde puedo encontrar . . . ?
DOHN-deh PWEH-doh ehn-kohn-TRAHR

General Answers

I/he/she would like . . .
Quisiera . . .
kee-see-EHR-ah

I don't like . . .
No me gusta(n) . . .
noh meh GOO-stah(n)

a little bit/a lot
un poco/mucho
oon POH-koh/MOO-choh

I'm looking for . . .
Busco . . .
BOO-skoh

Appendix B

Spanish to English Dictionary

A

abogado/a   lawyer
ah-boh-GAH-doh/dah
abolladura   dent
ah-boh-yah-DOO-rah
abrigo   coat
ah-BREE-goh
abuela   grandmother
ah-BWEH-lah
abril   April
ah-BREEHL
abuelo   grandfather
ah-BWEH-loh
aceite   oil
ah-SAY-teh
acera   sidewalk
ah-SEH-rah
actor/actriz   actor
ahk-TOHR ahk-TREEHS
actual   current
ahk-too-AHL
adelante   ahead
ah-deh-LAHN-teh
aduana   customs
ah-DWAH-nah
agente de policía   police officer
ah-HEN-teh deh poh-lee-SEE-yah
(el) agua   water
ehl AH-gwah
(el) agua caliente   water, hot
ehl AH-gwah kah-lee-EHN-teh

(el) agua con gas   water, carbonated
ehl AH-gwah kohn gahs
(el) agua fría   water, cold
ehl AH-gwah FREE-ah
(el) agua mineral   mineral water
ehl AH-gwah mee-neh-RAHL
(el) agua sin gas   water, noncarbonated
ehl AH-gwah seen gahs
agosto   August
ah-GOHS-toh
(el) aguacate   avocado
ehl ah-gwah-KAH-teh
agrio   sour
AH-gree-oh
(el) aire acondicionado   air-conditioning
ehl AY-reh ah-kohn-dee-see-oh-NAH-doh
(el) albaricoque   apricot
ehl ahl-bah-ree-KOH-keh
(el) álbum   album
ehl AHL-boom
alcachofa   artichoke
ahl-kah-CHOH-fah
(el) alcohol   alcohol
ehl ahl-KOHL
alemán/ana   German
ah-leh-MAHN/MAHN-ah
alergia   allergy
ah-LEHR-hee-ah

(el) algodón	cotton
ehl ahl-goh-DOHN	
al lado de	next to
AHL LAH-doh deh	
(el) almacén	department store
ehl ahl-mah-SEHN	
almeja	clam
ahl-MEH-hah	
avena	oats
ah-VEH-nah	
(las) aves de corral	poultry
lahs AH-vehs deh koh-RAHL	
almuerzo	lunch
ahl-MWEHR-soh	
alpaca	alpaca
ahl-PAH-kah	
alquilar	to rent
ahl-kee-LAHR	
el alquiler de coches	car rental
ehl ahl-kee-LEHR deh KOH-chehs	
(la) altitud	altitude
lah ahl-tee-TOOD	
amarillo	yellow
ah-mah-REE-yoh	
americano/a	American
ah-mehr-ee-CAH-noh/nah	
amigo/a	friend
ah-MEE-goh/gah	
ancho	loose
AHN-choh	
anchoa	anchovy
ahn-CHOH-ah	
(el) andén	platform
ehl ahn-DEHN	
angora	angora
ahn-GOH-rah	
anguila	eel
ahn-GEE-lah	
anticuario	antique shop
ahn-tee-KWAH-ree-oh	
anillo	ring
ah-NEE-yoh	
(el) ante	suede
ehl AHN-teh	
aorta	aorta
ah-OHR-tah	
aperitivo	appetizer
ah-peh-ree-TEE-boh	

apio	celery
AH-pee-oh	
argentino/a	Argentinean
ahr-hen-TEE-noh/nah	
(el) arroz	rice
ehl ah-RROHS	
(el) arroz con leche	rice pudding
ehl ah-RROHS kohn LEH-cheh	
arteria	artery
ahr-teh-REE-ah	
artista	artist
ahr-TEE-stah	
asado	baked, roasted
ah-SAH-doh	
asiento	seat
ah-see-EHN-toh	
asistir	to attend
ah-sees-TEEHR	
(el) asma	asthma
ehl AHS-mah	
(el) ataque de apoplejía	stroke
ehl ah-TAH-keh deh ah-poh-pleh-HEE-ah	
(el) ataque al corazón	heart attack
ehl ah-TAH-keh ahl koh-rah-SOHN	
atender	to serve
ah-tehn-DEHR	
(el) aterrizaje	landing
ehl ah-teh-rree-SAH-heh	
a través de	through
ah trah-VEHS deh	
(el) atún	tuna
ehl ah-TOON	
(los) auriculares	headphones
lohs ow-ree-koo-LAH-rehs	
australiano/a	Australian
ow-strah-lee-AH-noh/nah	
(el) autobús	bus
ehl ow-toh-BOOS	
avería	breakdown
ah-veh-REE-ah	
(el) avión	airplane
ehl ah-vee-OHN	
axila	armpit
AHK-see-lah	
azafato/a	flight attendant
ah-sah-FAH-toh/tah	
azul	blue
ah-SOOL	

B

bacalao   cod
bah-kah-LAOH

bailarín/ina   dancer
bahy-lah-REEN/REEN-ah

bajo   short (not tall)
BAH-hoh

banana   banana
bah-NAH-nah

bañera   bathtub
bah-NYEH-rah

baño   bathroom
BAHN-yoh

barra de pan   bread, loaf of
BAH-rrah deh pahn

(el) bar   bar
ehl bahr

barato   inexpensive
bah-RAH-toh

barba   beard
BAHR-bah

barbería   barbershop
bahr-beh-REE-ah

batido   milk shake
bah-TEE-doh

beige   beige
behj

berenjena   eggplant
beh-rehn-HEH-nah

bien asado   well-done
bee-EHN ah-SAH-doh

(el) bigote   mustache
ehl bee-GOH-teh

(el) billete   ticket
ehl bee-YEH-teh

billete de primera clase   first class ticket
bee-YEH-teh deh pree-MEH-rah KLAH-seh

biografía   biography
bee-oh-grah-FEE-ah

(el) bistec   steak
ehl bee-STEHK

bizarro   brave
bee-SAH-roh

blanco   white
BLAHN-koh

blusa   blouse
BLOO-sah

boca   mouth
lah BOH-kah

bocadillo   sandwich (on a roll)
boh-kah-DEE-yoh

bollo   dinner roll
BOH-yoh

una bolsa de   a bag of
OO-nah BOHL-sah deh

bombero/a   firefighter
bohm-BEH-roh/rah

bonito/a   pretty
boh-NEE-toh/ah

bota   boot
BOH-tah

una botella de   a bottle of
OO-nah boh-TEH-yah deh

bragas   panties
BRAH-gahs

brazo   arm
BRAH-soh

(el) brécol   broccoli
ehl BREH-kohl

brocha   paintbrush
BROH-chah

Buenas noches   Good evening
BWEH-nas NOH-ches

Buenas tardes   Good afternoon
BWEH-nas TAHR-dehs

Buenos días   Good morning
BWEH-nos DEE-yahs

bufanda   scarf
boo-FAHN-dah

C

cachemira   cashmere
kah-cheh-MEE-rah

(el) café)   coffee
ehl kah-FEH

una caja de   a box of
OO-nah KAH-hah deh

caja de seguridad   a safe
KAH-hah deh seh-goo-ree-DAHD

(el) calabacín   zucchini
ehl kah-lah-bah-SEEN

calabaza   squash
kah-lah-BAH-sah

(los) calcetines socks
lohs kahl-seh-TEE-nehs

calculadora calculator
kahl-koo-lah-DOHR-ah

café brown
kah-FEH

caliente hot
kah-lee-EHN-teh

(la) calle street
KAH-yeh

calzoncillos men's underpants
kahl-sohn-SEE-ohs

cama bed
KAH-mah

cama individual bed, twin
KAH-mah een-dee-vee-doo-AHL

cama matrimonial bed, double
KAH-mah mah-tree-moh-nee-AHL

cámara camera
KAH-mah-rah

cámara de video video camera
KAH-mah-rah deh bee-DEY-oh

camarero bartender, waiter
kah-mah-REH-roh

camarera waitress
kah-mah-REH-rah

cambio de dinero money exchange
CAHM-bee-oh deh dee-NEH-roh

camisa shirt
kah-MEE-sah

camiseta t-shirt
kah-mee-SEH-tah

canadiense Canadian
cah-nah-dee-YEHN-seh

(la) canción song
lah kahn-see-OHN

cangrejo crab
kahn-GREH-hoh

cantante singer
kahn-TAHN-teh

cara face
KAH-rah

caramelos candy
kah-rah-MEH-lohs

(la) carne meat
KAHR-neh

(la) carne de cerdo pork
lah KAHR-neh deh SEHR-doh

(la) carne de cordero lamb
lah KAHR-neh deh kohr-DEH-roh

(la) carne de ternera veal
lah KAHR-neh deh tehr-NEHR-ah

(la) carne de vaca beef
lah KAHR-neh deh BAH-kah

carnicería butcher shop
kahr-nee-seh-REE-ah

caro expensive
KAH-roh

carretera highway
kah-reh-TEH-rah

carta menu
KAHR-tah

cebolla onion
seh-BOH-yah

cerebro brain
seh-REH-broh

(el) carné de conducir driver's license
ehl kahr-NEH deh kohn-doo-SEER

carrito cart
ehl kah-REE-toh

cartero/a postal worker
kahr-TEH-roh/rah

ceja eyebrow
SEH-hah

cena dinner
SEH-nah

cerca near
SEHR-kah

(los) cereales grains
lohs seh-reh-AH-lehs

(el) cereal del desayuno breakfast cereal
ehl seh-reh-AHL dehl deh-sahy-OO-noh

cereza cherry
seh-REH-sah

cerveza beer
sehr-VEH-sah

chaleco vest
chah-LEH-koh

chaleco salvavidas life vest
chah-LEH-koh sahl-vah-VEE-dahs

(el) champán champagne
ehl chahm-PAHN

(el) champiñón mushroom
ehl chahm-peen-YOHN

(el) champú   shampoo
ehl chahm-POO

chaqueta   jacket
chah-KEH-tah

(el) cheque check (form of payment)
ehl CHEH-keh

chileno/a   Chilean
chee-LEH-noh/ah

chivo   goat
CHEE-voh

(el) chocolate   chocolate
ehl choh-koh-LAH-teh

(el) choque   car accident
ehl CHOH-keh

chorizo   sausage
choh-REE-soh

chuleta   cutlet
choo-LEH-tah

(el) cine   cinema
ehl SEE-neh

cinta   cassette tape
SEEN-tah

cinta adhesiva   tape
SEEN-tah ahd-heh-SEE-vah

moving walkway cintas transportadoras
SEEN-tahs trahns-pohr-tah-DOHR-ahs

(el) cinturón   belt
ehl seen-too-ROHN

ciruela   plum
see-roo-EH-lah

ciruela pasa   prune
see-roo-EH-lah PAH-sah

claro   light
KLAH-roh

clavo   nail
KLAH-boh

cobrador conductor, bill collector
koh-brah-DOHR

(el) coche   car
ehl KOH-cheh

cocinero/a   chef, cook
koh-see-NEH-roh/rah

coco   coconut
KOH-koh

(la) col   cabbage
lah kohl

(la) coliflor   cauliflower
lah koh-lee-FLOHR

(el) collar   necklace
ehl koh-YAHR

colmado   grocery store
kohl-MAH-doh

colombiano/a   Colombian
coh-lohm-bee-AH-noh/nah

conchas de peregrino   scallops
KOHN-chahs deh peh-reh-GREE-noh

conducir   to drive
kohn-doo-SEER

compromiso   commitment
kohm-proh-MEE-soh

(el) conductor   bus driver
ehl kohn-dook-TOHR

constipación   cold (a cold)
kohn-stee-pah-see-OHN

contable   accountant
kohn-TAH-bleh

copa de vino   wine glass
KOH-pah deh VEE-noh

copos de avena   oatmeal
KOH-pohs deh ah-VEH-nah

(el) corazón   heart
ehl koh-rah-SOHN

corbata   neck tie
kohr-BAH-tah

(el) cordón de zapato   shoelace
ehl kohr-DOHN deh sah-PAH-toh

(el) corte de pelo   haircut
ehl KOHR-teh deh PEH-loh

corto   short (not long)
KOHR-toh

costarricense   Costa Rican
coh-stah-rree-CEHN-seh

cremallera rota   broken zipper
creh-mah-YEHR-ah ROH-tah

(el) crespón   crepe
ehl krehs-POHN

crudo   raw
KROO-doh

cuaderno   notebook
kwah-DEHR-noh

cuarto   fourth, room
KWAHR-toh

cuarto de baño   bathroom
KWAHR-toh deh BAHN-yoh

cubierto place setting
koo-bee-EHR-toh

cubitos de hielo ice cubes
koo-BEE-tohs deh ee-YEHL-oh

cuchara spoon
coo-CHAH-rah

cuchara sopera soup spoon
coo-CHAH-rah soh-PEH-rah

cucharita teaspoon
coo-chah-REE-tah

cuello neck
KWEH-yoh

cuenta bill
KWEHN-tah

cuero leather
KWEH-roh

cuerpo body
KWEHR-poh

cuñado/a brother-in-law/sister-in-law
koo-NYAH-doh/dah

D

danés/esa Danish
dah-NEHS/NEHS-ah

el dátil date (fruit)
ehl DAH-teehl

decepción disappointment
deh-sehp-see-OHN

décimo tenth
DEH-see-moh

dedo finger
DEH-doh

dedo del pie toe
DEH-doh dehl pee-YEH

delgado thin
dehl-GAH-doh

demasiado grande too big
deh-mah-see-AH-doh GRAHN-deh

demasiado pequeño too small
deh-mah-see-YAH-doh peh-KEH-nyoh

dentista dentist
dehn-TEE-stah

depilación waxing
]deh-pee-lah-see-OHN

derecha right
deh-REH-chah

derecho straight, a right
deh-REH-choh

desayuno breakfast
deh-sahy-YOO-noh

(el) despegue take-off
ehl dehs-PEH-geh

detergente detergent
deh-tehr-HEN-teh

detrás de behind
deh-TRAHS deh

día day
DEE-ah

(el) diamante diamond
ehl dee-ah-MAHN-teh

diciembre December
dee-see-EHM-breh

(el) diente tooth
ehl dee-EHN-teh

dinero money
dee-NEH-roh

el disco compacto compact disc
ehl DEE-skoh kohm-PAHK-toh

(el) disquete computer disk
ehl dees-KEH-teh

doble turn
DOH-bleh

domingo Sunday
doh-MEEN-goh

dominicano/a Dominican
doh-mee-nee-CAH-noh/nah

dorado gold
doh-RAH-doh

(el) dril denim
ehl dreel

ducha shower
DOO-chah

dulce sweet
DOOL-she

E

ecuatoriano/a Ecuadorian
eh-cwah-toh-ree-AH-noh/nah

edificio building
eh-dee-FEE-see-yoh

efectivo cash
ehl eh-fehk-TEE-boh

egipcio/a Egyptian
eh-HEEP-see-yoh/yah

embarazada pregnant
ehm-bah-rah-SAH-dah

(el) empeine arch
ehl ehm-PEY-neh

empleado/a employee
ehm-pleh-YAH-doh/dah

(el) encaje lace
ehl ehn-KAH-heh

enero January
eh-NEH-roh

enfermero/a nurse
ehn-fehr-MEH-roh/rah

ensalada salad
ehn-sah-LAH-dah

entrada entrance, movie or
ehn-TRAH-dah theater ticket

(el) equipaje baggage
ehl eh-kee-PAH-heh

(el) equipaje extraviado lost baggage
ehl eh-kee-PAH-heh ehks-trah-bee-AH-doh

escalera de mano ladder
ehs-kah-LEH-rah deh MAH-noh

escena stage
eh-SEH-nah

escribir a máquina to type
ehs-kree-BEER ah MAH-kee-nah

escritor/a writer
eh-scree-TOHR/TOHR-ah

escritorio desk
oon ehs-kree-TOHR-ee-oh

escuela school
eh-SKWEH-lah

esmeralda emerald
ehs-meh-RAHL-dah

espalda back
eh-SPAHL-dah

español/a Spanish
eh-spah-NYOHL/NYOHL-ah

espárragos asparagus
ehs-PAH-rrah-gohs

la espinaca spinach
eh-spee-NAH-kah

esposo/a husband/wife
ehs-POH-soh/sah

esqueleto skeleton
eh-SKEH-leh-toh

esquina street corner
eh-SKEE-nah

(la) estación season
lah eh-stah-see-OHN

(la) estación de metro metro station
lah eh-stah-see-YOHN deh MEH-troh

estanquillo tobacco shop
eh-stahn-KEE-yoh

estar to be
ehs-TAHR

este east
EHS-teh

estrecho tight
eh-STREH-choh

estudiante student
eh-stoo-dee-AHN-teh

europeo/a European
eh-oo-roh-PEH-oh/ah

éxito success
EHK-see-toh

(las) exposiciones exposures
lahs ehks-poh-see-see-OHN-ehs

F

falda skirt
FAHL-dah

farmacia pharmacy
la fahr-MAH-see-ah

farmacéutico/a pharmacist
fahr-mah-SEH-OO-tee-coh/cah

(el) fax fax machine
ehl fahks

febrero February
feh-BREHR-oh

feo ugly
FEH-oh

(la) ficción fiction
lah feek-see-OHN

fila row
FEE-lah

filipino/a Filipino/a
fee-lee-PEE-noh/nah

fino thin
FEE-noh

flequillo bangs
fleh-KEE-yoh

fosa nasal nostril
FOH-sah nah-SAHL

fotocopiadora photocopier
foh-toh-koh-pee-ah-DOH-rah

frambuesa raspberry
frahm-BWEH-sah

francés/a frahn-SEHS/SEHS-ah	French
(la) frente lah FREHN-teh	forehead
fresa FREH-sah	strawberry
fresca FREHS-kah	fresh
(los) frijoles lohs free-HOH-lehs	beans
frío FREE-oh	cold
frito FREE-toh	fried
fruta FROO-tah	fruit

G

galleta gah-YEH-tah	cookie
gambas GAHM-bahs	shrimp
garbanzos gahr-BAHN-sohs	chickpeas
gaseosa gah-seh-OH-sah	soda
gasolina gah-soh-LEE-nah	gasoline
gerente heh-REHN-teh	manager
gimnasio heem-NAH-see-oh	gym
goma GOH-mah	eraser, rubber
gorro GOH-rroh	cap
grande GRAHN-deh	large
grapadora grah-pah-DOHR-ah	stapler
grasa GRAH-sah	fat
gris grees	gray
grueso groo-EH-soh	thick
(los) guantes lohs GWAHN-tehs	gloves

guayaba gwah-YAH-bah	guava
(los) guisantes lohs gee-SAHN-tehs	peas
guitarrista ghee-tah-RREE-stah	guitarist

H

(la) habitación lah ah-bee-tah-see-OHN	room
hamburguesa ahm-boor-GEH-sah	hamburger
harina ah-REE-nah	flour
helado eh-LAH-doh	ice cream
heladería eh-lah-deh-REE-ah	ice cream shop
hermana/o ehr-MAH-nah/noh	sister/brother
hermanastra/o ehr-mah-NAHS-trah/troh	stepsister/stepbrother
hígado HEE-gah-doh	liver
higo EE-goh	fig
hija/o EE-hah/hoh	daughter/son
hijastra/o ee-HAS-trah/oh	stepdaughter/stepson
Hola OH-lah	Hello
holandés/esa oh-lahn-DEHS/DEHS-ah	Dutch
hondureño/a ohn-doo-REH-nyoh/nyah	Honduran
horario oh-RAH-ree-oh	schedule
(el) hostal ehl ohs-STAHL	hostel
(el) hotel ehl oh-TEHL	hotel
hoy oy	today
hueco WEH-koh	hole

hueso bone
WEH-soh
huevo egg
WEH-voh

I

impresora printer
eem-preh-SOH-rah
ingeniero/a engineer
een-heh-nee-EH-roh/rah
inglés English
een-GLEHS
invierno winter
een-bee-YEHR-noh
iraní Iranian
ee-rah-NEE
iraquí Iraqi
ee-RAH-kee
irlandés/esa Irish
eer-lahn-DEHS/DEHS-ah
italiano/a Italian
ee-tahl-ee-AH-noh/nah
izquierda left
eehs-kee-YEHR-dah

J

(el) jamón ham
ehl hah-MOHN
jefe/a boss
HEH-feh/fah
(el) jerez sherry
ehl heh-REHS
joyería jewelry store
hoy-eh-REE-ah
joyero/a jeweler
hoh-YEH-roh/rah
judías green beans
hoo-DEE-ahs
jueves Thursday
HWEH-vehs
jugo juice
HOO-goh
julio July
HOO-lee-oh
junio June
HOO-nee-oh

K, L

labio lip
LAH-bee-oh
lámpara lamp
LAHM-pah-rah
lana wool
LAH-nah
langosta lobster
lahn-GOHS-tah
(el) lápiz pencil
ehl LAH-pees
largo long
LAHR-goh
lata can
LAH-tah
lavabo sink
lah-VAH-boh
lavadora washing machine
lah-vah-DOHR-ah
lavandería Laundromat
lah-vahn-dehr-EE-ah
(la) leche milk
lah LEH-cheh
lechuga lettuce
leh-CHOO-gah
lejía bleach
leh-HEE-ah
lejos far
LEH-hos
lengua tongue
LEHN-gwah
lentejas lentils
lehn-TEH-hahs
lima lime
LEE-mah
(el) limón lemon
lee-MOHN
lenguado sole (fish)
lehn-GWAH-doh
libre de impuestos duty free
LEE-breh deh eem-PWEH-stohs
librería bookstore
lee-breh-REE-ah
libro book
LEE-broh
libro para niños children's book
LEE-broh PAH-rah NEE-nyohs

lino linen
LEE-noh

literatura no novelesca nonfiction
lee-teh-rah-TOO-rah noh noh-veh-LEH-skah

lomo fino filet mignon
LOH-moh FEE-noh

lunes Monday
LOO-nehs

luz light
loos

LL

(la) llave key
YAH-veh

llegada arrival
yeh-GAH-dah

M

madrastra stepmother
mah-DRAHS-trah

madre mother
MAH-dreh

(el) maíz corn
ehl mah-EES

mancha stain
MAHN-chah

mango mango
MAHN-goh

manicura manicure
mah-nee-KOO-rah

(el) mantel tablecloth
ehl mahn-TEHL

mantequilla butter
mahn-teh-KEE-yah

manzana apple, street block
mahn-SAH-nah

mañana tomorrow
mah-NYAH-nah

máquina de billetes ticket machine
MAH-kee-nah deh bee-YEH-tehs

marinero/a sailor
mah-ree-NEH-roh/rah

marisco shellfish
mah-REE-skoh

marrón brown
mah-ROHN

martes Tuesday
MAHR-tehs

marzo March
MAHR-soh

mayo May
MAH-yoh

mecánico/a mechanic
meh-CAH-nee-coh/cah

mediano medium
meh-dee-AH-noh

medias stockings
MEH-dee-ahs

médico/a doctor
MEH-dee-coh/cah

mejilla cheek
meh-HEE-yah

(el) mejillón mussel
ehl meh-hee-YOHN

mejor better
meh-HOHR

(el) melocotón peach
ehl meh-loh-koh-TOHN

(el) melón melon
ehl meh-LOHN

(el) mensaje message
ehl mehn-SAH-heh

merienda snack
meh-ree-EHN-dah

merluza bass
mehr-LOO-sah

(el) mes month
ehl mehs

mesa table
MEH-sah

metro subway
MEH-troh

mexicano/a Mexican
meh-hee-CAH-noh/nah

miércoles Wednesday
mee-EHR-koh-lehs

mirtilo blueberry
meer-TEE-loh

molestar to bother
moh-lehs-TAHR

morado purple
moh-RAH-doh

mucho a lot
MOO-choh

músculo muscle
MOO-skoo-loh

muselina muslin
moo-seh-LEE-nah

música music
MOO-see-kah

músico/a musician
MOO-see-coh/cah

N

naranja orange
nah-RAHN-hah

(la) nariz nose
lah nah-REES

nata cream
NAH-tah

nectarina nectarine
nehk-tah-REE-nah

negro black
NEH-groh

nervio nerve
NEHR-bee-oh

nicaragüense Nicaraguan
nee-cah-rah-GWEN-seh

nieta/o granddaughter/grandson
nee-EH-tah

(el) nilon nylon
ehl NEE-lohn

norte north
NOHR-teh

norteamericano/a North American
nohr-teh-ah-mehr-ee-CAH-noh/nah

noruego/a Norwegian
nohr-WEH-goh/gah

novela novel
noh-VEH-lah

noveno ninth
noh-VEH-noh

novia/o girlfriend/boyfriend
NOH-vee-ah/oh

noviembre November
noh-vee-EHM-breh

O

octavo eighth
ohk-TAH-voh

octubre October
ohk-TOO-breh

oeste west
ooh-EHS-teh

ojo eye
OH-hoh

ondulado wavy
ohn-doo-LAH-doh

(el) ordenador computer
ehl ohr-deh-nah-DOHR

oreja ear
oh-REH-hah

órgano organ
OHR-gah-noh

oro gold
OH-roh

oscuro dark
oh-SKOO-roh

ostra oyster
OHS-trah

otoño fall
oh-TOH-nyoh

P

padrastro stepfather
pah-DRAHS-troh

padre father
PAH-dreh

pagar to pay
PAH-gahr

palomitas popcorn
pah-loh-MEE-tahs

(el) pan bread
ehl pahn

(el) pan integral whole wheat bread
ehl pahn een-teh-GRAHL

pan y mantequilla bread and butter
pahn ee mahn-teh-KEE-yah

(el) pan tostado toast
ehl pahn toh-STAH-doh

pana corduroy
PAH-nah

panadería bakery
pah-nah-deh-REE-ah

pantalla movie screen
pahn-TAH-yah

(los) pantalones pants
lohs pahn-tah-LOH-nehs

(los) pantalones cortos shorts
lohs pahn-tah-LOH-nehs COR-tohs

pantimedias pahn-tee-MEH-dee-ahs	pantyhose	**película** peh-LEE-koo-lah	camera film, motion picture
papa PAH-pah	potato	**pelo** PEH-loh	hair
(el) papel ehl pah-PEHL	paper	**(los) pendientes** lohs pehn-dee-EHN-tehs	earrings
(el) papel higiénico ehl pah-PEHL ee-HYEHN-ee-koh	toilet paper	**peor** peh-YOHR	worse
parada de autobús pah-RAH-dah deh ow-toh-BOOS	bus stop	**pepino** peh-PEE-noh	cucumber
parada de taxis pah-RAH-dah deh TAHK-sees	taxi stand	**pequeño** peh-KEH-nyoh	small
paraguayo/a pah-rah-GOOAHY-oh/ah	Paraguayan	**pera** PEH-rah	pear
(a la) parrilla ah lah pah-REE-yah	grilled	**percha** PEHR-chah	hanger
párpado PAHR-pah-doh	eyelid	**periódico** peh-ree-OH-dee-koh	newspaper
pasa PAH-sah	raisin	**periodista** peh-ree-oh-DEE-stah	journalist
(el) pasaporte ehl pah-sah-POHR-teh	passport	**la permanente** lah pehr-mah-NEHN-teh	perm
(el) pase de abordar ehl PAH-seh deh ah-bohr-DAHR	boarding card	**peruano/a** peh-roo-AH-noh/nah	Peruvian
pasillo pah-SEE-yoh	aisle	**pescadería** peh-skah-deh-REE-ah	fish shop
(el) pastel ehl pah-STEHL	pie	**pescado** pehs-KAH-doh	fish
pastelería pah-steh-leh-REE-ah	pastry shop	**pestaña** peh-STAH-nyah	eyelash
patillas pah-TEE-yahs	sideburns	**(el) pez espada** ehl pehs eh-SPAH-dah	swordfish
pato PAH-toh	duck	**pianista** pee-ah-NEE-stah	pianist
pavo PAH-voh	turkey	**picado** pee-KAH-doh	chopped
(el) peaje ehl peh-AH-heh	toll	**picante** pee-KAHN-teh	spicy
pecho PEH-choh	chest	**(el) pie** ehl pee-YEH	foot
pedicura peh-dee-KOO-rah	pedicure	**(la piel)** lah pee-EHL	skin
pegamento peh-gah-MEHN-toh	glue	**pierna** pee-YEHR-nah	leg
peinado pey-NAH-doh	hairstyle	**pila** PEE-lah	battery
peinar pey-NAHR	to comb	**piloto/a** pee-LOH-toh/tah	pilot

pimiento — pepper
pee-mee-EHN-toh

pincho de — a bit of
PEEN-choh deh

pintor/a — painter
peen-TOHR/TOHR-ah

pintura — paint
peen-TOO-rah

piña — pineapple
PEEN-yah

piscina — swimming pool
pee-SEE-nah

piso — floor
PEE-soh

pista de baile — dance floor
PEE-stah deh BAHY-leh

plata — silver
PLAH-tah

plátano — plantain
PLAH-tah-noh

platino — platinum
plah-TEE-noh

plato — plate
PLAH-toh

plato principal — entree
PLAH-toh preen-see-PAHL

pluma — pen
PLOO-mah

(un) poco — a little bit
oon POH-koh deh

poco cocido — rare
POH-koh coh-SEEH-doh

poesía — poetry
poh-eh-SEE-ah

polaco/a — Polish
poh-LAH-coh/cah

(el) poliéster — polyester
poh-lee-EHS-tehr

pollo — chicken
POH-yoh

polvo — dust
POHL-boh

pomelo — grapefruit
poh-MEH-loh

(el) portaequipajes — baggage compartment
ehl pohr-tah-eh-kee-PAH-hehs

portero — doorman
pohr-TEH-roh

(el) postre — dessert
ehl POHS-treh

precio del viaje — fare
PREH-see-oh dehl vee-AH-heh

pretender — to try
preh-tehn-DEHR

primavera — spring
pree-mah-VEHR-ah

primero — first
pree-MEHR-oh

primo/a — cousin
PREE-moh/mah

productos lácteos — dairy
pro-DUHK-tohs LAHK-teh-ohs

profesor/a — teacher, professor
proh-feh-SOHR/SOHR-ah

prometido/a — fiancé/ée
proh-meh-TEE-doh/ah

propina — tip
proh-PEE-nah

prueba — test
proo-EH-bah

(el) pudín — pudding
ehl poo-DEEN

(el) puente — bridge
ehl PWEHN-teh

puerta de embarque — boarding gate
PWEHR-tah deh ehm-BAHR-keh

puertorriqueño/a — Puerto Rican
pwehr-toh-rree-KEH-nyoh/nyah

(el) pulgar — thumb
ehl pool-GAHR

pulsera — bracelet
pool-SEH-rah

Q

quemado — burned
keh-MAH-doh

queso — cheese
KEH-soh

quinto — fifth
KEEN-toh

R

ración de — an order of
rah-see-OHN deh

(el) rasgón   tear
ehl RAHS-gohn

rayado   striped
rah-YAH-doh

(el) rayón   rayon
ehl rah-YOHN

(la) reacción alérgica   allergic reaction
lah reh-ahk-see-OHN ah-LEHR-hee-kah

rebanada de pan   slice of bread
reh-bah-NAH-dah deh pahn

(la) reclamación de equipajes   baggage claim
lah reh-klah-mah-see-OHN deh eh-kee-PAH-hehs

recordar   to remember
reh-kohr-DAHR

(el) recorte   trim (hair)
ehl reh-KOHR-teh

redactor/a   editor
reh-dahk-TOHR/TOHR-ah

reflejos   highlights (hair)
reh-FLEH-hohs

remolacha   beet
reh-moh-LAH-chah

(la) reservación   reservation
lah rehs-ehr-vah-see-OHN

revista   magazine
reh-BEE-stah

rizada   kale
ree-SAH-dah

rizado   curly
ree-SAH-doh

rodilla   knee
roh-DEE-yah

rojo   red
ROH-hoh

(el) ron   rum
ehl rohn

ropa   clothing
ROH-pah

ropa interior   underwear
ROH-pah een-teh-ree-OHR

rosa   rose
ROH-sah

rosado   rose (color)
roh-SAH-doh

(el) rosbif   roast beef
ehl rohs-BEEHF

roto/a   broken
ROH-toh/tah

(el) rubí   ruby
ehl roo-BEE

ruso/a   Russian
ROO-soh/sah

S

sábado   Saturday
SAH-bah-doh

sábana   sheet
SAH-bah-nah

(el) sacapuntas   pencil sharpener
ehl sah-kah-POON-tahs

saco   sack
SAH-koh deh

salchicha   hot dog
sahl-CHEE-chah

salchichonería   delicatessen
sahl-chee-choh-neh-REE-ah

salida   departure
sah-LEE-dah

salida de emergencia   emergency exit
sah-LEE-dah deh eh-mehr-HEN-see-ah

(el) salmón   salmon
sahl-MOHN

(el) salón de belleza   beauty salon
ehl sah-LOHN deh beh-YEH-sah

salteado   sautéed
sahl-teh-AH-doh

salvado   bran
sahl-BAH-doh

salvadoreño/a   El Salvadoran
sahl-vah-doh-REH-nyoh/nyah

sandalias   sandals
sahn-DAH-lee-ahs

sandía   watermelon
sahn-DEE-ah

(el) sandwich   sandwich (on sliced bread)
ehl sahn-WEECH

(la) sangre   blood
lah SAHN-greh

ser   to be
sehr

sano   healthy
SAH-noh

(el) secador de pelo   hairdryer
ehl seh-kah-DOHR deh PEH-loh

secadora   clothes dryer
seh-kah-DOHR-ah

secar el pelo   blow dry
seh-KAHR ehl PEH-loh

secretario/a   secretary
seh-kreh-TAH-ree-yoh/yah

seda   silk
SEH-dah

segundo   second
seh-GOON-doh

seguro   insurance
seh-GOO-roh

sello   stamp
SEH-yoh

señas   directions
las SEH-nyahs

Señor   Sir
seh-NYOHR

Señora   Mrs.
seh-NYOH-rah

Señorita   Miss
seh-nyoh-REE-tah

septiembre   September
sehp-tee-EHM-breh

séptimo   seventh
SEHP-tee-moh

servilleta   napkin
sehr-vee-YEH-tah

sexto   sixth
SEHS-toh

sigue   continue
SEE-geh

simpático   nice
seem-PAH-tee-koh

(el) sobre   envelope
ehl SOH-breh

sobrina/o   niece/nephew
soh-BREE-nah/noh

soldado   soldier
sohl-DAH-doh

sombrero   hat
sohm-BREH-roh

sopa   soup
SOH-pah

(el) soplete   blowtorch
ehl soh-PLEH-teh

soso   bland
SOH-soh

(el) sostén   bra
ehl sohs-TEHN

sudamericano/a   South American
sood-ah-meh-ree-CAH-noh/nah

suegra/o   mother-in-law/father-in-law
SWEH-grah/groh

suela   sole (of the shoe)
SWEH-lah

(el) sujetapapeles   paperclip
ehl soo-HEH-tah-pah-PEHL-ehs

supermercado   supermarket
soo-pehr-mehr-KAH-doh

sur   south
soor

T

(el) tacón   heel
ehl tah-KOHN

taquilla   ticket window
tah-KEE-yah

tarjeta postal   postcard
tahr-HEH-tah POH-stahl

tarro   jar
TAH-rroh

(el) taxi   taxi
ehl TAHK-see

(el) taxista   taxi driver
ehl tahk-SEES-tah

taza   cup
TAH-sah

(el) tazón   bowl
ehl tah-SOHN

(el) té   tea
ehl teh

teatro   theater
teh-AH-troh

techo   ceiling
TEH-choh

teléfono   telephone
teh-LEH-foh-noh

(la) televisión   television
lah teh-leh-vee-see-OHN

(el) tenedor   fork
ehl teh-neh-DOHR

tercero   third
tehr-SEH-roh

terciopelo velvet
TEHR-see-oh-PEH-loh

tía/o aunt/uncle
TEE-ah/oh

(el) tiburón shark
ehl tee-boo-ROHN

tienda de fotografía camera shop
tee-EHN-dah deh foh-toh-grah-FEE-ah

tienda de discos record store
tee-EHN-dah deh DEES-kohs

tienda de ropa clothing store
tee-EHN-dah deh ROH-pah

tintorería dry cleaner's
teen-toh-rehr-EE-ah

toalla towel
toh-AY-yah

toalla de baño bath towel
toh-AY-yah deh BAH-nyoh

toalla para la cara face towel
toh-AY-yah PAH-rah lah KAH-rah

toalla para las manos hand towel
toh-AY-yah PAH-rah lahs MAH-nohs

(el) tomate tomato
ehl toh-MAH-teh

topacio topaz
toh-PAH-see-yoh

torta cake
TOHR-tah

tostado toasted
toh-STAH-doh

trabajo job
trah-BAH-hoh

tráfico traffic
TRAH-fee-koh

(el) traje suit
ehl TRAH-heh

(el) traje de baño bathing suit
ehl TRAH-heh deh BAH-nyoh

trigo wheat
TREE-goh

trucha trout
TROO-chah

turquesa turquoise
toor-KEH-sah

U

uva grape
OO-bah

V

(al) vapor steamed
ahl vah-POHR

vaqueros jeans, cowboys
vah-KEH-rohs

vaso glass
VAH-soh

vecino/a neighbor
veh-SEE-noh/nah

vendedor/a salesman/woman
vehn-deh-DOHR/DOHR-ah

ventana window
vehn-TAH-nah

verano summer
vehr-AH-noh

verde green
VEHR-deh

verdura vegetable
vehr-DOO-rah

vestido dress
veh-STEE-doh

viernes Friday
vee-EHR-nehs

vino wine
VEE-noh

vuelo flight
VWEH-loh

W, Y, Z

(el) wáter toilet
ehl WAH-tehr

(el) yogur yogurt
ehl yoh-GOOR

zafiro sapphire
sah-FEE-roh

zanahoria carrot
sah-nah-OH-ree-ah

zapatería shoe store
sah-pah-teh-REE-ah

zapato shoe
sah-PAH-toh

Appendix C

English to Spanish Dictionary

A

accountant	**contable**
	kohn-TAH-bleh
across from	**a través de**
	ah trah-VEHS deh
actor	**actor**
	ahk-TOHR
actress	**actriz**
	ahk-TREEHS
ahead	**adelante**
	ah-deh-LAHN-teh
air-conditioning	**aire acondicionado**
	AY-reh ah-kohn-dee-see-oh-NAH-doh
airplane	**avión**
	ah-vee-OHN
aisle	**pasillo**
	pah-SEE-yoh
album	**álbum**
	AHL-boom
alcohol	**alcohol**
	ehl ahl-KOHL
allergy	**alergia**
	ah-LEHR-hee-ah
allergic reaction	**reacción alérgica**
	reh-ahk-see-OHN ah-LEHR-hee-kah
alpaca	**alpaca**
	ahl-PAH-kah
a lot	**mucho**
	MOO-choh
altitude	**altitud**
	ahl-tee-TOOD

American	**americano/a**
	ah-mehr-ee-CAH-noh/nah
anchovy	**anchoa**
	ahn-CHOH-ah
angora	**angora**
	ahn-GOH-rah
antique shop	**anticuario**
	ahn-tee-KWAH-ree-oh
aorta	**aorta**
	ah-OHR-tah
appetizer	**aperitivo**
	ah-peh-ree-TEE-voh
apple	**manzana**
	mahn-SAH-nah
apricot	**albaricoque**
	ahl-bah-ree-KOH-keh
April	**abril**
	ah-BREEHL
arch	**empeine**
	ehl ehm-PEY-neh
Argentinean	**argentino/a**
	ahr-hen-TEE-noh/nah
arm	**brazo**
	BRAH-soh
armpit	**axila**
	AHK-see-lah
arrival	**llegada**
	yeh-GAH-dah
artery	**arteria**
	ahr-teh-REE-ah
artichoke	**alcachofa**
	ahl-kah-CHOH-fah
artist	**artista**
	ahr-TEE-stah

THE EVERYTHING SPANISH PHRASE BOOK

asparagus	**espárragos**	battery	**pila**
	ehs-PAH-rrah-gohs		PEE-lah
asthma	**asma**	to be	**estar, ser**
	AHS-mah		eh-STAR, sehr
to attend	**asistir**	beans	**frijoles**
	ah-sees-TEEHR		free-HOH-lehs
August	**agosto**	beard	**barba**
	ah-GOHS-toh		BAHR-bah
Australian	**australiano/a**	beauty salon	**salón de belleza**
	ow-strah-lee-AH-noh/nah		sah-LOHN deh beh-YEH-sah
aunt	**tía**	bed	**cama**
	TEE-ah		KAH-mah
avocado	**aguacate**	bed, double	**cama matrimonial**
	ah-gwah-KAH-teh		KAH-mah mah-tree-moh-nee-AHL
		bed, twin	**cama individual**
B			KAH-mah een-dee-vee-doo-AHL
back	**espalda**	beef	**carne de vaca**
	eh-SPAHL-dah		KAHR-neh deh VAH-kah
a bag of	**una bolsa de**	beer	**cerveza**
	OO-nah BOHL-sah deh		sehr-VEH-sah
baggage	**equipaje**	beet	**remolacha**
	eh-kee-PAH-heh		reh-moh-LAH-chah
baggage claim	**reclamación de equipajes**	belt	**cinturón**
reh-klah-mah-see-OHN deh eh-kee-PAH-hehs			seen-too-ROHN
baggage compartment	**portaequipajes**	better	**mejor**
pohr-tah-eh-kee-PAH-hehs			meh-HOHR
baked	**asado**	behind	**detrás de**
	ah-SAH-doh		deh-TRAHS deh
bakery	**panadería**	beige	**beige**
	pah-nah-deh-REE-ah		behj
banana	**banana**	bill	**cuenta**
	bah-NAH-nah		KWEHN-tah
bangs	**flequillo**	biography	**biografía**
	fleh-KEE-yoh		bee-oh-grah-FEE-ah
bar	**bar**	a bit of	**un pincho de**
	bahr		oon PEEN-choh deh
barbershop	**barbería**	black	**negro**
	bahr-beh-REE-ah		NEH-groh
bartender	**camarero**	bland	**soso**
	kah-mah-REH-roh		SOH-soh
bass	**merluza**	bleach	**lejía**
	mehr-LOO-sah		leh-HEE-ah
bathing suit	**traje de baño**	block	**manzana**
	TRAH-heh deh BAHN-yoh		mahn-SAH-nah
bathroom	**cuarto de baño**	blood	**sangre**
	KWAHR-toh deh BAHN-yoh		SAHN-greh
bathtub	**bañera**	blouse	**blusa**
	bah-NYEH-rah		BLOO-sah

blow dry	**secar el pelo**
	seh-KAHR ehl PEH-loh
blowtorch	**soplete**
	soh-PLEH-teh
blue	**azul**
	ah-SOOL
blueberry	**mirtilo**
	meer-TEE-loh
boarding card	**pase de abordar**
	PAH-seh deh ah-bohr-DAHR
body	**cuerpo**
	KWEHR-poh
boarding gate	**puerta de embarque**
	PWEHR-tah deh ehm-BAHR-keh
a bottle of	**una botella de**
	OO-nah boh-TEHY-yah deh
bone	**hueso**
	WEH-soh
book	**libro**
	LEE-broh
bookstore	**librería**
	lee-breh-REE-ah
boot	**bota**
	BOH-tah
boss	**jefe/a**
	HEH-fe/fa
bother, to	**molestar**
	moh-lehs-TAHR
bowl	**tazón**
	tah-SOHN
a box of	**una caja de**
	OO-nah KAH-hah deh
boyfriend	**novio**
	NOH-vee-oh
bra	**sostén**
	sohs-TEHN
bracelet	**pulsera**
	pool-SEH-rah
brain	**cerebro**
	seh-REH-broh
bran	**salvado**
	sahl-BAH-doh
brave	**bizarro**
	bee-SAHR-roh
breakfast	**desayuno**
	ehl deh-sahy-YOO-noh

breakfast cereal	**cereal del desayuno**
	seh-ree-AHL dehl deh-sahy-OO-noh
bread	**pan**
	pahn
bread and butter	**pan y mantequilla**
	pahn ee mahn-teh-KEE-yah
bread, loaf of	**barra de pan**
	BAH-rrah deh pahn
bread, slice of	**rebanada de pan**
	reh-bah-NAH-dah deh pahn
bread, whole wheat	**pan integral**
	ehl pahn een-teh-GRAHL
breakdown	**avería**
	ah-veh-REE-ah
bridge	**puente**
	PWEHN-teh
broccoli	**brécol**
	BREH-kohl
broken	**roto/a**
	ROH-toh/tah
broken zipper	**cremallera rota**
	creh-mah-YEHR-ah ROH-tah
brother	**hermano**
	ehr-MAH-noh
brother-in-law	**cuñado**
	koo-NYAH-doh
brown	**marrón, café**
	mah-RROHN, kah-FEH
building	**edificio**
	eh-dee-FEE-see-yoh
burned	**quemado**
	keh-MAH-doh
bus	**autobús**
	ow-toh-BOOS
bus driver	**conductor**
	kohn-dook-TOHR
bus stop	**parada de autobús**
	pah-RAH-dah deh ow-toh-BOOS
butcher shop	**carnicería**
	kahr-nee-seh-REE-ah
butter	**mantequilla**
	mahn-teh-KEE-yah

C

cabbage	**col**
	kohl
cake	**torta**
	TOHR-tah

calculator	**calculadora**	cheese	**queso**
	kahl-koo-lah-DOHR-ah		KEH-soh
camera	**cámara**	chef	**cocinero/a**
	KAH-mah-rah		koh-see-NEH-roh/rah
camera film	**película**	cherry	**cereza**
	peh-LEE-koo-lah		seh-REH-sah
camera shop	**tienda de fotografía**	chest	**pecho**
	tee-EHN-dah deh foh-toh-grah-FEE-ah		PEH-choh
a can of	**una lata de**	chicken	**pollo**
	OO-nah LAH-tah deh		POH-yoh
Canadian	**canadiense**	chickpeas	**garbanzos**
	cah-nah-dee-EHN-seh		gahr-BAHN-sohs
candy	**caramelos**	children's book	**libro para niños**
	kah-rah-MEH-lohs		LEE-broh PAH-rah NEE-nyohs
cantaloupe	**melón**	Chilean	**chileno/a**
	meh-LOHN		chee-LEH-no/a
cap	**gorro**	chocolate	**chocolate**
	GOH-rroh		choh-koh-LAH-teh
car	**coche**	chopped	**picado**
	KOH-cheh		pee-KAH-doh
car accident	**choque**	cinema	**cine**
	CHOH-keh		SEE-neh
car rental	**alquiler de coches**	clam	**almeja**
	ahl-kee-LEHR deh KOH-chehs		ahl-MEH-hah
carrot	**zanahoria**	clothes dryer	**secadora**
	sah-nah-OH-ree-ah		seh-kah-DOHR-ah
cart	**carrito**	clothing	**ropa**
	kah-RREE-toh		ROH-pah
cash	**efectivo**	clothing store	**tienda de ropa**
	eh-fehk-TEE-boh		tee-EHN-dah deh ROH-pah
cashmere	**cachemira**	coat	**abrigo**
	kah-cheh-MEE-rah		ah-BREE-goh
cassette tape	**cinta**	coconut	**coco**
	SEEN-tah		KOH-koh
cauliflower	**coliflor**	cod	**bacalao**
	koh-lee-FLOHR		bah-kah-LAOH
ceiling	**techo**	coffee	**café**
	TEH-choh		kah-FEH
celery	**apio**	cold	**frío**
	AH-pee-oh		FREE-oh
champagne	**champán**	cold (a cold)	**constipación**
	chahm-PAHN		kohn-stee-pah-see-OHN
check (bill)	**cuenta**	Colombian	**colombiano/a**
	KWEHN-tah		coh-lohm-bee-AH-noh/nah
check (form of payment)	**cheque**	to comb	**peinar**
	CHEH-keh		pey-NAHR
cheek	**mejilla**	commitment	**compromiso**
	meh-HEE-yah		kohm-proh-MEE-soh

compact disc   **disco compacto**
DEE-skoh kohm-PAHK-toh

computer   **computadora/ordenador**
cohm-poo-tah-DOH-rah/ohr-deh-nah-DOHR

conductor   **cobrador**
koh-brah-DOHR

continue   **sigue**
SEE-geh

cookie   **galleta**
gah-YEH-tah

corduroy   **pana**
PAH-nah

corn   **maíz**
mah-EES

Costa Rican   **costarricense**
coh-stah-rree-SEHN-seh

cotton   **algodón**
ahl-goh-DOHN

cousin   **primo/a**
PREE-moh/mah

crab   **cangrejo**
kahn-GREH-hoh

cream   **nata**
NAH-tah

crepe   **crespón**
krehs-POHN

cross   **cruce**
KROO-seh

Cuban   **cubano/a**
coo-BAH-noh/nah

cucumber   **pepino**
peh-PEE-noh

cup   **taza**
TAH-sah

curly   **rizado**
ree-SAH-doh

current   **actual**
ahk-too-AHL

customs   **aduana**
ah-DWAH-nah

cutlet   **chuleta**
choo-LEH-tah

D

dairy   **productos lácteos**
pro-DUHK-tohs LAHK-teh-ohs

dance floor   **pista de baile**
PEE-stah deh BAHY-leh

dancer   **bailarín/ina**
bahy-lah-REEN/REEN-ah

Danish   **danés/esa**
dah-NEHS/NEHS-ah

dark   **oscuro**
oh-SKOO-roh

date   **dátil**
DAH-teehl

daughter   **hija**
EE-hah

day   **día**
DEE-ah

December   **diciembre**
dee-see-EHM-breh

delicatessen   **salchichonería**
sahl-chee-choh-neh-REE-ah

denim   **dril**
dreel

dent   **abolladura**
ah-boh-yah-DOO-rah

dentist   **dentista**
dehn-TEE-stah

department store   **almacén**
ahl-mah-SEHN

departure   **salida**
sah-LEE-dah

desk   **escritorio**
ehs-kree-TOHR-ee-oh

dessert   **postre**
POHS-treh

detergent   **detergente**
deh-tehr-HEN-teh

diamond   **diamante**
dee-ah-MAHN-teh

dinner   **cena**
SEH-nah

dinner roll   **bollo**
BOH-yoh

directions   **señas**
SEH-nyahs

disappointment   **decepción**
deh-sehp-see-OHN

disk   **disquete**
dees-KEH-teh

doctor   **médico/a**
MEH-dee-coh/cah

Dominican	dominicano/a
	doh-mee-nee-CAH-noh/nah
doorman	portero
	pohr-TEH-roh
dress	vestido
	veh-STEE-doh
to drive	conducir
	kohn-doo-SEER
driver's license	carné de conducir
	kahr-NEH deh kohn-doo-SEER
dry cleaner's	tintorería
	teen-toh-rehr-EE-ah
duck	pato
	PAH-toh
dust	polvo
	POHL-voh
Dutch	holandés/esa
	oh-lahn-DEHS/DEHS-a
duty free	libre de impuestos
	LEE-breh deh eem-PWEH-stohs

E

east	este
	EHS-teh
ear	oreja
	oh-REH-hah
earrings	pendientes
	pehn-dee-EHN-tehs
Ecuadorian	ecuatoriano/a
	eh-cwah-toh-ree-AH-noh/nah
editor	redactor/a
	reh-dahk-TOHR/TOHR-ah
eel	anguila
	ahn-GEE-lah
egg	huevo
	ehl WEH-voh
eggplant	berenjena
	beh-rehn-HEH-nah
Egyptian	egipcio/a
	eh-HEEP-see-yoh/yah
eighth	octavo
	ohk-TAH-voh
elevator	ascensor
	ah-sehn-SOHR
Salvadoran	salvadoreño/a
	sahl-vah-doh-REH-nyoh/nyah
emergency exit	salida de emergencia
	sah-LEE-dah deh eh-mehr-HEN-see-ah

emerald	esmeralda
	ehs-meh-RAHL-dah
engineer	ingeniero/a
	een-heh-nee-EH-roh/rah
employee	empleado/a
	ehm-pleh-AH-doh/dah
English	inglés
	een-GLEHS
entrance	entrada
	ehn-TRAH-dah
entree	plato principal
	PLAH-toh preen-see-PAHL
envelope	sobre
	SOH-breh
eraser	goma
	GOH-mah
European	europeo/a
	eh-oo-roh-PEH-oh/ah
exit	salida
	sah-LEE-dah
expensive	caro
	KAH-roh
exposures	exposiciones
	ehs-poh-see-see-OHN-ehs
eye	ojo
	OH-hoh
eyebrow	ceja
	SEH-hah
eyelash	pestaña
	peh-STAH-nyah
eyelid	párpado
	PAHR-pah-doh

F

face	cara
	KAH-rah
fall	otoño
	oh-TOH-nyoh
far	lejos
	LEH-hos
fare	precio del viaje
	PREH-see-oh dehl vee-AH-heh
fat	grasa
	GRAH-sah
father	padre
	PAH-dreh
father-in-law	suegro
	SWEH-groh

fax machine	**fax**
	fahks
February	**febrero**
	feh-BREHR-oh
fiance/ee	**prometido/a**
	proh-meh-TEE-do/a
fiction	**ficción**
	feek-see-OHN
fifth	**quinto**
	KEEN-toh
fig	**higo**
	EE-goh
filet mignon	**lomo fino**
	LOH-moh FEE-noh
Filipino/a	**filipino/a**
	fee-lee-PEE-noh/nah
finger	**dedo**
	DEH-doh
firefighter	**bombero/a**
	bohm-BEH-roh/rah
first	**primero**
	pree-MEHR-oh
first class ticket	**billete de primera clase**
bee-YEH-teh deh pree-MEH-rah KLAH-seh	
fish	**pescado**
	pehs-KAH-doh
fish shop	**pescadería**
	peh-skah-deh-REE-ah
flight	**vuelo**
	VWEH-loh
flight attendant	**azafato/a**
	ah-sah-FAH-toh/tah
flight number	**número de vuelo**
NOO-meh-roh deh VWEH-lo	
floor	**piso**
	PEE-soh
flour	**harina**
	ah-REE-nah
foot	**pie**
	pee-EH
forehead frente	
	FREHN-teh
fork	**tenedor**
	teh-neh-DOHR
form of	**forma de identificación**
identification FOHR-mah deh ee-dehn-tee-fee-kah-see-OHN	

fourth	**cuarto**
	KWAHR-toh
French	**francés/esa**
	frahn-SEHS/SEHS-ah
fresh	**fresca**
	FREHS-kah
Friday	**viernes**
	vee-EHR-nehs
fried	**frito**
	FREE-toh
fruit	**fruta**
	FROO-tah
friend	**amigo/a**
	ah-MEE-goh/gah

G

gasoline	**gasolina**
	gah-soh-LEE-nah
German	**alemán/ana**
	ah-leh-MAHN/MAHN-ah
girlfriend	**novia**
	NOH-vee-ah
glass	**vaso**
	VAH-soh
gloves	**guantes**
	GWAHN-tehs
glue	**pegamento**
	peh-gah-MEHN-toh
goat	**chivo**
	CHEE-voh
go back	**vuelve**
	VWEHL-veh
go down	**baje**
	BAH-heh
go past	**pase**
	PAH-seh
go up	**sube**
	SOO-beh
gold	**oro**
	ehl OH-roh
golden	**dorado**
	doh-RAH-doh
good afternoon	**buenas tardes**
	BWEH-nas TAHR-dehs
good evening	**buenas noches**
	BWEH-nas NOH-ches
good morning	**buenos días**
	BWEH-nos DEE-ahs

grains	cereales	hat	sombrero
	seh-reh-AH-lehs		sohm-BREH-roh
granddaughter	nieta	headphones	auriculares
	nee-EH-tah		ow-ree-koo-LAH-rehs
grandfather	abuelo	healthy	sano
	ah-BWEH-loh		SAH-noh
grandmother	abuela	heart	corazón
	ah-BWEH-lah		koh-rah-SOHN
grandson	nieto	heart attack	ataque al corazón
	nee-EH-toh		ah-TAH-keh ahl koh-rah-SOHN
grape	uva	heel	tacón
	OO-vah		tah-KOHN
grapefruit	pomelo	hello	hola
	poh-MEH-loh		OH-lah
gray	gris	highlights	reflejos
	grees		reh-FLEH-hohs
green	verde	highway	carretera
	VEHR-deh		kah-reh-TEH-rah
green beans	judías	hole	hueco
	hoo-DEE-ahs		WEH-koh
grilled	a la parrilla	Honduran	hondureño/a
	ah lah pah-REE-yah		ohn-doo-REH-nyoh/nyah
grocery store	colmado	hostel	hostal
	kohl-MAH-doh		ohs-STAHL
guava	guayaba	hot	caliente
	gwah-YAH-bah		kah-lee-EHN-teh
guitarist	guitarrista	hot chocolate	chocolate caliente
	gee-tah-RREE-stah		choh-koh-LAH-teh kah-lee-EHN-teh
gym	gimnasio	hot dog	salchicha
	heem-NAH-see-oh		sahl-CHEE-chah
		hotel	hotel
H			oh-TEHL
		husband	esposo, marido
hair	pelo		ehs-POH-soh, mah-REE-doh
	PEH-loh		
a haircut	un corte de pelo	**I**	
	oon KOHR-teh deh PEH-loh		
hairdryer	secador de pelo	ice cream	helado
	seh-kah-DOHR deh PEH-loh		eh-LAH-doh
hairstyle	peinado	ice cream shop	heladería
	pey-NAH-doh		eh-lah-deh-REE-ah
ham	jamón	ice cubes	cubitos de hielo
	hah-MOHN		koo-BEE-tohs deh ee-YEHL-oh
hamburger	hamburguesa	I'm going to . . .	Voy a . . .
	ahm-boor-GEH-sah		vohy ah
hanger	percha	inexpensive	barato
	PEHR-chah		bah-RAH-toh
hallway	pasillo	insurance	seguro
	pah-SEE-yoh		seh-GOO-roh

Iranian	**iraní**	**lamp**	**lámpara**
	ee-RAH-nee		LAHM-pah-rah
Iraqi	**iraquí**	**landing**	**aterrizaje**
	ee-RAH-kee		ah-teh-rree-SAH-heh
Irish	**irlandés/esa**	**large**	**grande**
	eer-lahn-DEHS/DEHS-ah		GRAHN-deh
Italian	**italiano/a**	**larger**	**más grande**
	ee-tahl-ee-AH-no/na		mahs GRAHN-deh
		Laundromat	**lavandería**
J			lah-vahn-dehr-EE-ah
jacket	**chaqueta**	**lawyer**	**abogado/a**
	chah-KEH-tah		ah-boh-GAH-doh/dah
January	**enero**	**leather**	**cuero**
	eh-NEH-roh		KWEH-roh
a jar of	**un tarro de**	**left**	**izquierda**
	oon TAH-rroh deh		eehs-kee-EHR-dah
jeans	**vaqueros**	**leg**	**pierna**
	vah-KEH-rohs		pee-EHR-nah
jeweler	**joyero/a**	**lemon**	**limón**
	hoh-YEH-roh/rah		lee-MOHN
jewelry store	**joyería**	**lentils**	**lentejas**
	hoy-eh-REE-ah		lehn-TEH-hahs
job	**trabajo**	**less expensive**	**más barato**
	trah-BAH-hoh		mahs bah-RAH-toh
journalist	**periodista**	**lettuce**	**lechuga**
	peh-ree-oh-DEE-stah		leh-CHOO-gah
July	**julio**	**life vest**	**chaleco salvavidas**
	HOO-lee-oh		chah-LEH-koh sahl-vah-VEE-dahs
juice	**jugo**	**light**	**luz**
	HOO-goh		loos
June	**junio**	**light**	**claro**
	HOO-nee-oh		KLAH-roh
		lime	**lima**
K			LEE-mah
kale	**rizada**	**linen**	**lino**
	ree-SAH-dah		LEE-noh
key	**llave**	**lip**	**labio**
	YAH-veh		LAH-bee-yoh
knee	**rodilla**	**a little bit**	**un poco de**
	roh-DEE-yah		oon POH-koh deh
		liver	**hígado**
L			HEE-gah-doh
lace	**encaje**	**lobster**	**langosta**
	ehn-KAH-heh		lahn-GOHS-tah
ladder	**escalera de mano**	**long**	**largo**
	ehs-kah-LEH-rah deh MAH-noh		LAHR-goh
lamb	**carne de cordero**	**longer**	**más largo**
	KAHR-neh deh kohr-DEH-roh		mahs LAHR-goh

loose **ancho**
AHN-choh

lost baggage **equipaje extraviado**
eh-kee-PAH-heh ehks-trah-vee-AH-doh

lost and found **oficina de**
objetos perdidos
oh-fee-SEE-nah deh ohb-HEH-tohs pehr-
DEE-dohs

lunch **almuerzo**
ahl-MWEHR-soh

M

magazine **revista**
reh-VEE-stah

manager **gerente**
heh-REHN-teh

mango **mango**
MAHN-goh

a manicure **una manicura**
OO-nah mah-nee-KOO-rah

March **marzo**
MAHR-soh

May **mayo**
MAH-yoh

meat **carne**
KAHR-neh

mechanic **mecánico/a**
meh-CAH-nee-coh/cah

medium **mediano**
meh-dee-AH-noh

melon **melón**
meh-LOHN

menu **carta, menú**
KAHR-tah, meh-NOO

message **mensaje**
mehn-SAH-heh

Mexican **mexicano/a**
meh-hee-CAH-no/na

metro station **estación de metro**
eh-stah-see-OHN deh MEH-troh

milk **leche**
LEH-cheh

milk shake **batido**
bah-TEE-doh

mineral water **agua mineral**
AH-gwah mee-neh-RAHL

Miss **Señorita**
seh-nyoh-REE-tah

missing button **botón perdido**
boh-TOHN pehr-DEE-doh

Monday **lunes**
LOO-nehs

money **dinero**
dee-NEH-roh

money exchange **cambio de dinero**
CAHM-bee-oh deh dee-NEH-roh

month **mes**
mehs

mother **madre**
MAH-dreh

mother-in-law **suegra**
SWEH-grah

mouth **boca**
BOH-kah

movie screen **pantalla**
pahn-TAHY-yah

movie ticket **entrada**
ehn-TRAH-dah

moving walkway cintas transportadoras
SEEN-tahs trahns-pohr-tah-DOHR-ahs

Mrs. **Señora**
seh-NYOH-rah

muscle **músculo**
MOO-skoo-loh

musician **músico/a**
MOO-see-coh/cah

mushroom **champiñon**
chahm-peen-YOHN

music **música**
MOO-see-kah

muslin **muselina**
moo-seh-LEE-nah

mussel **mejillón**
meh-hee-YOHN

mustache **bigote**
bee-GOH-teh

N

nail **clavo**
KLAH-voh

napkin **servilleta**
sehr-vee-YEH-tah

near **cerca**
SEHR-kah

neck **cuello**
KWEH-yoh

necklace **collar**
koh-YAHR

nectarine **nectarina**
nehk-tah-REE-nah

neighbor **vecino/a**
veh-SEE-noh/nah

nephew **sobrino**
soh-BREE-noh

nerve **nervio**
NEHR-vee-oh

newspaper **periódico**
ehl peh-ree-OH-dee-koh

next to **al lado de**
ahl LAH-doh deh

Nicaraguan **nicaragüense**
nee-cah-rah-GWEN-seh

nice **simpático**
seem-PAH-tee-koh

niece **sobrina**
soh-BREE-nah

ninth **noveno**
noh-BEH-noh

nonfiction **literatura no novelesca**
lee-teh-rah-TOO-rah noh noh-veh-LEH-skah

north **norte**
NOHR-teh

North American **norteamericano/a**
nohr-teh-ah-mehr-ee-CAH-noh/nah

Norwegian **noruego/a**
nohr-WEH-goh/gah

nose **nariz**
nah-REES

nostril **fosa nasal**
FOH-sah nah-SAHL

notebook **cuaderno**
kwah-DEHR-noh

novel **novela**
noh-VEH-lah

November **noviembre**
noh-vee-EHM-breh

nurse **enfermero/a**
ehn-fehr-MEH-roh/rah

nylon **nilon**
NEE-lohn

O

oatmeal **copos de avena**
KOH-pohs deh ah-VEH-nah

oats **avena**
ah-VEH-nah

October **octubre**
ohk-TOO-breh

oil **aceite**
ah-SAY-teh

one-way ticket **billete sencillo**
bee-YEH-teh sehn-SEE-yoh

onion **cebolla**
seh-BOH-yah

orange **naranja**
nah-RAHN-hah

an order of **una ración de**
OON-ah rah-see-OHN deh

organ **órgano**
OHR-gah-noh

oyster **ostra**
OHS-trah

P

paint **pintura**
peen-TOO-rah

paintbrush **brocha**
BROH-chah

painter **pintor/a**
peen-TOHR/TOHR-ah

panties **bragas**
BRAH-gahs

pants **pantalones**
pahn-tah-LOH-nehs

pantyhose **pantimedias**
pahn-tee-MEH-dee-ahs

paper **papel**
pah-PEHL

paperclip **sujetapapeles**
soo-HEH-tah-pah-PEHL-ehs

Paraguayan **paraguayo/a**
pah-rah-GWAY-oh/ah

passport **pasaporte**
pah-sah-POHR-teh

pastry shop **pastelería**
pah-steh-leh-REE-ah

to pay **pagar**
PAH-gahr

peach	**melocotón/durazno**
	meh-loh-koh-TOHN/doo-RAHS-noh
pear	**pera**
	PEH-rah
peas	**guisantes**
	gee-SAHN-tehs
a pedicure	**una pedicura**
	OO-nah peh-dee-KOO-rah
pen	**pluma**
	PLOO-mah
pencil	**lápiz**
	LAH-pees
pepper (condiment)	**pimienta**
	pee-mee-EHN-tah
pepper (vegetable)	**pimiento**
	pee-mee-EHN-toh
pencil sharpener	**sacapuntas**
	sah-kah-POON-tahs
perm	**permanente**
	pehr-mah-NEHN-teh
Peruvian	**peruano/a**
	peh-roo-AH-noh/nah
pharmacist	**farmacéutico/a**
	fahr-mah-SEH-OO-tee-coh/cah
pharmacy	**farmacia**
	fahr-MAH-see-ah
photocopier	**fotocopiadora**
	foh-toh-koh-pee-ah-DOH-rah
pianist	**pianista**
	pee-ah-NEE-stah
pie	**pastel**
	pah-STEHL
pillow	**almohada**
	ahl-moh-AH-dah
pilot	**piloto/a**
	pee-LOH-toh/tah
pineapple	**piña**
	PEEN-yah
pink	**rosado**
	roh-SAH-doh
place setting	**cubierto**
	koo-bee-EHR-toh
plantain	**plátano**
	PLAH-tah-noh
plate	**plato**
	PLAH-toh
platform	**andén**
	ahn-DEHN

platinum	**platino**
	plah-TEE-noh
plum	**ciruela**
	see-roo-EH-lah
poetry	**poesía**
	poh-eh-SEE-ah
police officer	**agente de policía**
	ah-HEN-teh deh poh-lee-SEE-ah
Polish	**polaco/a**
	poh-LAH-coh/cah
polyester	**poliéster**
	poh-lee-EHS-tehr
popcorn	**palomitas**
	pah-loh-MEE-tahs
pork	**carne de cerdo**
	KAHR-neh deh SEHR-doh
postal worker	**cartero/a**
	kahr-TEH-roh/rah
postcard	**tarjeta postal**
	tahr-HEH-tah POH-stahl
potato	**papa**
	PAH-pah
poultry	**aves de corral**
	AH-vehs deh koh-RRAHL
prune	**ciruela pasa**
	see-roo-EH-lah PAH-sah
pregnant	**embarazada**
	ehm-bah-reh-SAH-dah
pretty	**bonito**
	boh-NEE-toh
printer	**impresora**
	eem-preh-SOH-rah
pudding	**pudín**
	poo-DEEN
Puerto Rican	**puertorriqueño/a**
	pwehr-toh-rree-KEH-nyoh/nyah
purple	**morado**
	moh-RAH-doh

R

raisin	**pasa**
	PAH-sah
rare	**poco cocido**
	POH-koh coh-SEE-doh
raspberry	**frambuesa**
	frahm-BWEH-sah
raw	**crudo**
	KROO-doh

rayon	**rayón**
	rah-YOHN
record store	**tienda de discos**
	tee-EHN-dah deh DEES-kohs
red	**rojo**
	ROH-hoh
to remember	**recordar**
	reh-kohr-DAHR
to rent	**alquilar**
	ahl-kee-LAHR
reservation	**reservación**
	rehs-ehr-vah-see-OHN
restrooms	**baños**
	BAHN-yohs
rice	**arroz**
	ah-RROHS
rice pudding	**arroz con leche**
	ah-RROHS kohn LEH-cheh
right	**derecha**
	deh-REH-chah
ring	**anillo**
	ah-NEE-yoh
roast beef	**rosbíf**
	rohs-BEEHF
room	**habitación**
	ah-bee-tah-see-OHN
round-trip ticket	**billete de ida y vuelta**
	bee-YEH-teh deh EE-dah ee VWEHL-tah
roasted	**asado**
	ah-SAH-doh
row	**fila**
	FEE-lah
ruby	**rubí**
	roo-BEE
rum	**ron**
	rohn
Russian	**ruso/a**
	ROO-soh/sah

S

a sack of	**un saco de**
	oon SAH-koh deh
a safe	**caja de seguridad**
	KAH-hah deh seh-goo-ree-DAHD
sailor	**marinero/a**
	mah-ree-NEH-roh/rah
salad	**ensalada**
	ehn-sah-LAH-dah
salesman/woman	**vendedor/a**
	vehn-deh-DOHR/DOHR-ah
salmon	**salmón**
	sahl-MOHN
sandals	**sandalias**
	sahn-DAH-lee-ahs
sandwich (on a roll)	**bocadillo**
	boh-kah-DEE-yoh
sandwich (on sliced bread)	**sandwich**
	sahn-WEECH
sapphire	**zafiro**
	sah-FEE-roh
Saturday	**sábado**
	SAH-bah-doh
sausage	**chorizo**
	choh-REE-soh
sautéed	**salteado**
	sahl-teh-AH-doh
scallops	**conchas de peregrino**
	KOHN-chahs deh peh-reh-GREE-noh
scarf	**bufanda**
	boo-FAHN-dah
schedule	**horario**
	oh-RAH-ree-oh
school	**escuela**
	eh-SKWEH-lah
scuff	**raya**
	RAH-yah
season	**estación**
	eh-stah-see-OHN
seat	**asiento**
	ah-see-EHN-toh
second	**segundo**
	seh-GOON-doh
second class ticket	**billete de segunda clase**
	bee-YEH-teh deh seh-GOON-dah KLAH-seh
secretary	**secretario/a**
	seh-kreh-TAH-ree-yoh/yah
September	**septiembre**
	sehp-tee-EHM-breh
to serve	**atender**
	ah-tehn-DEHR
seventh	**séptimo**
	SEHP-tee-moh
shampoo	**champú**
	chahm-POO

shark	**tiburón**	skeleton	**esqueleto**
	tee-boo-ROHN		eh-SKEH-leh-toh
sheet	**sábana**	skin	**piel**
	SAH-bah-nah		pee-EHL
shellfish	**marisco**	skirt	**falda**
	mah-REE-skoh		FAHL-dah
sherry	**jerez**	small	**pequeño**
	heh-REHS		peh-KEH-nyoh
shirt	**camisa**	smaller	**más pequeño**
	kah-MEE-sah		mahs peh-KEH-nyoh
shoe	**zapato**	snack	**merienda**
	sah-PAH-toh		meh-ree-EHN-dah
shoelace	**cordón de zapato**	socks	**calcetines**
	kohr-DOHN deh sah-PAH-toh		kahl-seh-TEE-nehs
shoe store	**zapatería**	soda	**gaseosa**
	sah-pah-teh-REE-ah		gah-seh-OH-sah
short (not tall)	**bajo**	soldier	**soldado**
	BAH-hoh		sohl-DAH-doh
short (not long)	**corto**	sole (fish)	**lenguado**
	KOHR-toh		lehn-GWAH-doh
shorter	**más corto**	sole (of the shoe)	**suela**
	mahs KOHR-toh		SWEH-lah
shorts	**pantalones cortos**	son	**hijo**
	pahn-tah-LOH-nehs KOHR-tos		EE-hoh
shower	**ducha**	song	**canción**
	DOO-chah		kahn-see-OHN
shrimp	**gambas**	soup	**sopa**
	GAHM-bahs		SOH-pah
sideburns	**patillas**	south	**sur**
	pah-TEE-yahs		soor
sidewalk	**acera**	soup spoon	**cuchara sopera**
	ah-SEH-rah		coo-CHAH-rah soh-PEH-rah
silk	**seda**	sour	**agrio**
	SEH-dah		AH-gree-oh
silver	**plata**	South American	**sudamericano/a**
	PLAH-tah		sood-ah-meh-ree-CAH-noh/nah
singer	**cantante**	Spanish	**español/a**
	kahn-TAHN-teh		eh-spah-NYOHL/NYOHL-a
sink	**lavabo**	spicy	**picante**
	lah-VAH-boh		pee-KAHN-teh
Sir	**Señor**	spinach	**espinaca**
	seh-NYOHR		eh-spee-NAH-kah
sister	**hermana**	spoon	**cuchara**
	ehr-MAH-nah		coo-CHAH-rah
sister-in-law	**cuñada**	spring	**primavera**
	koo-NYAH-dah		pree-mah-VEHR-ah
sixth	**sexto**	squash	**calabaza**
	SEKS-toh		kah-lah-BAH-sah

stage	escena eh-SEH-nah	suede	ante AHN-teh
stain	mancha MAHN-chah	suit	traje TRAH-heh
stamp	sello SEH-yoh	summer	verano vehr-AH-noh
stapler	grapadora grah-pah-DOHR-ah	Sunday	domingo doh-MEEN-goh
stationery store	papelería pah-peh-leh-REE-ah	supermarket	supermercado soo-pehr-mehr-KAH-doh
steak	bistec bee-STEHK	sweet	dulce DOOL-seh
steamed	al vapor ahl vah-POHR	swimming pool	piscina pee-SEE-nah
stepbrother	hermanastro ehr-mah-NAHS-troh	swordfish	pez espada pehs eh-SPAH-dah
stepdaughter	hijastra ee-HAS-trah	**T**	
stepfather	padrastro pah-DRAHS-troh	t-shirt	camiseta kah-mee-SEH-tah
stepmother	madrastra mah-DRAHS-trah	table	mesa MEH-sah
stepsister	hermanastra ehr-mah-NAHS-trah	tablecloth	mantel mahn-TEHL
stepson	hijastro ee-HAS-troh	take	tome TOH-meh
stockings	medias MEH-dee-ahs	take-off	despegue dehs-PEH-geh
stop here	pare aquí PAH-reh ah-KEE	tape	cinta adhesiva SEEN-tah ahd-heh-SEE-vah
straight	derecho deh-REH-choh	taxi	taxi TAHK-see
strawberry	fresa FREH-sah	taxi driver	taxista tahk-SEES-tah
street	calle KAH-yeh	taxi stand	parada de taxis pah-RAH-dah deh TAHK-sees
street corner	esquina eh-SKEE-nah	teacher	profesor/a proh-feh-SOHR/SOHR-ah
striped	rayado rah-YAH-doh	tear	rasgón RAHS-gohn
stroke	ataque de apoplejía ah-TAH-keh deh ah-poh-pleh-HEE-ah	tea	té teh
student	estudiante eh-stoo-dee-AHN-teh	teaspoon	cucharita coo-chah-REE-tah
subway	metro MEH-troh	telephone	teléfono teh-LEH-foh-noh
success	éxito EHK-see-toh	television	televisión teh-leh-vee-see-OHN

tenth	**décimo**		**tongue**	**lengua**
	DEH-see-moh			LEHN-gwah
test	**prueba**		**too big**	**demasiado grande**
	proo-EH-bah			deh-mah-see-YAH-doh GRAHN-deh
theater	**teatro**		**too small**	**demasiado pequeño**
	teh-AH-troh			deh-mah-see-YAH-doh peh-KEH-nyoh
thick	**grueso**		**tooth**	**diente**
	groo-EH-soh			dee-YEHN-teh
thin	**delgado, fino**		**topaz**	**topacio**
	dehl-GAH-doh, FEE-noh			toh-PAH-see-yoh
third	**tercero**		**towel**	**toalla**
	tehr-SEH-roh			toh-AY-yah
thumb	**pulgar**		**towel, bath**	**toalla de baño**
	pool-GAHR			toh-AY-yah deh BAH-nyoh
Thursday	**jueves**		**towel, face**	**toalla para la cara**
	HWEH-vehs			toh-AY-yah PAH-rah lah KAH-rah
ticket	**billete**		**towel, hand**	**toalla para las manos**
	ehl bee-YEH-teh			toh-AY-yah PAH-rah lahs MAH-nohs
ticket machine	**máquina de billetes**		**trim**	**recorte**
	MAH-kee-nah deh bee-YAH-tehs			reh-KOHR-teh
ticket window	**taquilla**		**trout**	**trucha**
	tah-KEE-yah			TROO-chah
tie	**corbata**		**To try**	**pretender, tratar**
	kohr-BAH-tah			preh-tehn-DEHR, trah-TAHR
tight	**estrecho**		**traffic**	**tráfico**
	eh-STREH-choh			TRAH-fee-koh
tip	**propina**		**Tuesday**	**martes**
	proh-PEE-nah			MAHR-tehs
today	**hoy**		**tuna**	**atún**
	oy			ah-TOON
toast	**pan tostado**		**turkey**	**pavo**
	ehl pahn toh-STAH-doh			PAH-boh
toasted	**tostado**		**turn**	**doble**
	toh-STAH-doh			DOH-bleh
tobacco shop	**estanquillo**		**turquoise**	**turquesa**
	ehl eh-stahn-KEE-yoh			toor-KEH-sah
toe	**dedo del pie**		**to type**	**escribir a máquina**
	DEH-doh dehl pee-YEH			ehs-kree-BEER ah MAH-kee-nah
toilet	**wáter**		**U**	
	WAH-tehr			
toilet paper	**papel higiénico**		**ugly**	**feo**
	pah-PEHL ee-HYEHN-ee-koh			FEH-oh
toll	**peaje**		**uncle**	**tío**
	peh-AH-heh			TEE-oh
tomato	**tomate**		**underpants (for men)**	**calzoncillos**
	toh-MAH-teh			kahl-sohn-SEE-yohs
tomorrow	**mañana**		**underwear**	**ropa interior**
	mah-NYAH-nah			ROH-pah een-teh-ree-OHR

Uruguayan **uruguayo/a**
oo-roo-GWAY-oh/ah

V

veal **carne de ternera**
KAHR-neh deh tehr-NEHR-ah

vegetable **verdura**
vehr-DOO-rah

velvet **terciopelo**
TEHR-see-oh-PEH-loh

Venezuelan **venezolano/a**
veh-neh-soh-LAH-noh/nah

vest **chaleco**
chah-LEH-koh

video camera **cámara de video**
KAH-mah-rah deh vee-DEH-oh

W, Y, Z

waiter **camarero**
kah-mah-REH-roh

waitress **camarera**
kah-mah-REH-rah

walk **camine**
kah-MEE-neh

washing machine **lavadora**
lah-vah-DOHR-ah

water **agua**
AH-gwah

water, carbonated **agua con gas**
AH-gwah kohn gahs

water, cold **agua fría**
AH-gwah FREE-ah

water, hot **agua caliente**
AH-gwah kah-lee-EHN-teh

water, noncarbonated **agua sin gas**
AH-gwah seen gahs

watermelon **sandía**
sahn-DEE-ah

wavy **ondulado**
ohn-doo-LAH-doh

a waxing **una depilación**
oo-nah deh-pee-lah-see-OHN

Wednesday **miércoles**
mee-EHR-koh-lehs

well-done **bien cocido**
bee-EHN koh-SEE-doh

west **oeste**
oh-EHS-teh

wheat **trigo**
TREE-goh

white **blanco**
BLAHN-koh

wife **esposa**
ehs-POH-sah

window **ventana**
vehn-TAH-nah

wine **vino**
VEE-noh

wine glass **copa de vino**
KOH-pah deh VEE-noh

winter **invierno**
een-vee-EHR-noh

wool **lana**
LAH-nah

worse **peor**
peh-OHR

writer **escritor/a**
eh-scree-TOHR/TOHR-ah

yellow **amarillo**
ah-mah-REE-yoh

yogurt **yogur**
yoh-GOOR

zucchini **calabacín**
kah-lah-bah-SEEN

Index